OSPREY AIRCRAFT OF THE ACES • 28

French Aces of World War 2

2

SERIES EDITOR: TONY HOLMES

OSPREY AIRCRAFT OF THE ACES • 28

French Aces of World War 2

Barry Ketley

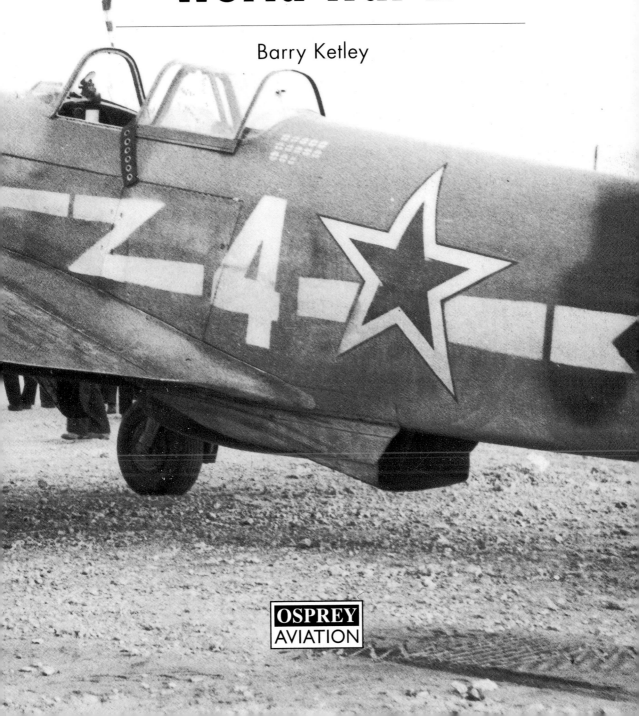

OSPREY
AVIATION

Front cover
This specially-commissioned cover artwork depicts an incident that took place on 29 September 1941 when *Sergent Chef Georges* Lemare of GC I/4 intercepted Gibraltar-based Short Sunderland N9044 'KG-C' of No 204 Sqn off the coast of Senegal. Lemare, based at Dakar-Oukam, was flying Curtiss Hawk '9', s/n 295, on this occasion. Although his gunfire stopped one of the flying boat's engines, the return fire lived up to the type's nickname of 'Flying Porcupine', and he was forced to break off the combat. Both aircraft returned safely to their respective bases. At the time this event took place, Lemare's score stood at four confirmed kills, including a Swordfish off Dakar almost a year previously. He did not finally make ace until 20 October 1944 while with the *Normandie-Niémen*, when he shot down an Fw 190. This was followed by eight more German fighters by 27 March 1945. Postwar, he entered civil aviation and was killed in the crash of a Bloch 161 on 26 January 1948. He was 30 years old (*cover artwork by Iain Wyllie*)

For a Catalogue of all books published by Osprey Aviation, Military and Automotive please write to:

The Marketing Manager, Osprey Publishing Ltd., P.O. Box 140, Wellingborough, Northants NN8 4ZA, United Kingdom
E-mail: info@OspreyDirect.co.uk

Osprey Direct USA, P.O. Box 130, Sterling Heights, MI 48311-0130, USA
E-mail: info@OspreyDirectUSA.com

OR VISIT THE OSPREY WEBSITE AT:
http://www.osprey-publishing.co.uk

First published in Great Britain in 1999 by Osprey Publishing, Elms Court, Chapel Way, Botley, Oxford, OX2 9LP

© 1999 Osprey Publishing Limited

ISBN 1 85532 898 4

Edited by Tony Holmes
Page design by TT Designs, T & B Truscott
Cover Artwork by Iain Wyllie
Aircraft Profiles by Mark Rolfe
Figure Artwork by Mike Chappell
Scale Drawings by Mark Rolfe
Origination by Grasmere Digital Imaging, Leeds, UK
Printed through Bookbuilders, Hong Kong

99 00 01 02 03   10 9 8 7 6 5 4 3 2 1

ACKNOWLEDGEMENTS
I wish to thank the following individuals/organisations for the provision of photographs – Phil Jarrett, Dick Ward, Bruce Robertson, Simon Parry, SHAA and ECPA.

EDITOR'S NOTE
To make this best-selling series as authoritative as possible, the editor would be extremely interested in hearing from any individual who may have relevant photographs, documentation or first-hand experiences relating to the elite pilots, and their aircraft, of the various theatres of war. Any material used will be fully credited to its original source. Please write to Tony Holmes at 10 Prospect Road, Sevenoaks, Kent, TN13 3UA, Great Britain.

CONTENTS

PRELUDE TO BLITZKRIEG

Without an understanding of the events which led to the Franco-German Armistice in June 1940, the conditions afterwards which directed French fighter pilots into combat against their allies – the British and Americans – and even their own countrymen, are difficult to understand. Consequently, some attention has been given to the operations and politics in France up until that time.

At the conclusion of World War 1, the French army and air forces were arguably the most powerful and best equipped in the world. Elated at redressing what was seen as the shame of the French defeat at the hands of the Prussians in 1870, and mourning the loss of nearly one-and-a-half million dead in the recent conflict, a vengeful France was in no mood to be magnanimous towards the defeated Germans. The consequence was the Treaty of Versailles, which imposed severe penalties upon the Germans. These penalties created bitter resentment in Germany, and therein lay the seeds of the far greater conflict which erupted in 1939.

Having won the 'war to end all wars', throughout the 1920s and 1930s, the military staffs of the victorious nations in Europe strove to develop a meaningful role for themselves. In Britain, this led to the development of a 'policing' role for the Royal Air Force, which was deemed necessary in order to control the sometimes recalcitrant populations of the Empire, and the development of some original thoughts on new forms of warfare, particularly involving armour.

A publicity photo of RAF Fairey Battles of No 88 Sqn of the AASF being escorted by Curtiss Hawks of GC I/5 'somewhere over France' during the 'Phoney War'. In reality, such Anglo-French missions occurred only rarely during the Battle of France

Two of the Czech pilots who flew with the *Armée de l'Air*, namely Tomas Vybiral (on left) and Josef Duda. The former scored seven confirmed kills in less than a month during the Battle of France while flying Curtiss Hawks with GC I/5. He later escaped to England and joined the RAF, where he was given command of No 312 Sqn in January 1943. Duda scored one victory with GC II/5. Note that Vybiral is wearing both Czech and French pilot's badges

In France, however, there seemed to be a stagnation in military thought, brought about by a climate of continuous political instability and parsimony. Even worse, the memories of the horrendous loss of life during 1914-18 seemed to create a 'siege' mentality, the result of which was the construction, at enormous expense, of the series of defensive Franco-German border fortifications known as the Maginot Line. This absorbed much of the military budget and slowed down the acquisition and development of newer hardware, particularly aircraft. Thus it was that as the French military establishment (many of whose most senior commanders were well past retirement age) sheltered behind their fortress walls, they not only failed to develop a coherent operational doctrine for their air force, the *Armée de l'Air*, but planned, in essence, to fight World War 1 all over again.

On 1 April 1933 (the same birthday being shared by the RAF) the *Aéronautique Militaire* became the *Armée de l'Air*, an independent arm of the French forces. Until this date the *Aéronautique Militaire* had enjoyed a similar relationship to the French army as had the Royal Flying Corps to the British army.

The Air Staff, recognising the decay into which the service had fallen, immediately began a series of planning studies to re-equip and reinvigorate the squadrons, but these were severely hampered by political and economic considerations.

By 1937 the consequences of these policies upon the *Armée de l'Air* were becoming plain for all to see. Although the force was equipped with substantial numbers of aircraft, most of these were obsolescent at best. As governments

Mainstay of the French fighter squadrons during 1939-40 was the Morane Saulnier MS.406. Overly complicated with many pneumatic systems, a single bullet could put it out of action

Adj Denis Ponteins of GC II/7 posing in front of his early production MS 406 which is fitted with the distinctive Bronzavia exhaust collectors. Ponteins scored six confirmed and one probable during the Battle of France before being seriously wounded. For the rest of the war he served with the Resistance

A magnificent 'pylone' executed by MS.406 No 169 (matricule militaire N489) of GC III/6 on 26 September 1939 at Chartres. The pilot, *Sgt* Grosdemanche, was unharmed. Such landings were not uncommon on the grass airfields of the period, most of which were little different to those used during World War 1

had formed and collapsed, reflecting the struggle between factions representing the extremes of Left and Right wing political thought, there had been no consistency in either policy or procurement of military equipment. Moreover, French industrial capacity had also been severely weakened through political instability. The worst example of this had been the badly-handled partial nationalisation of the aviation industry, which had begun in the summer of 1936 (at the very instant that Adolf Hitler had first revealed his hand by reoccupying the Rhineland).

Against this background, the best efforts of a series of very capable Ministers of Aviation saw only modest improvements made over the final years of the decade. Indeed, it was not until the summer of 1940 that truly modern aircraft began to reach the squadrons.

On 1 January 1937, the *Armée de l'Air* had 795 fighters on strength, of which only 278 were regarded as 'modern' – these were essentially variants of the fixed-undercarriage Dewoitine D.500 series. The various planning studies which had been started in 1933 culminated in 1938 in Plan V (5). Under this, the *Armée de l'Air* was to receive 1373 new-generation fighters, made up as follows:

16 Morane Saulnier MS.405s
1045 Morane Saulnier MS.406s
25 Bloch 150s
287 Potez 630/631 two-seat
  fighters

It was quickly recognised that this ambitious plan was beyond the capabilities of the French aircraft industry, which was riddled with inefficiency, industrial unrest and, on occasions, deliberate sabotage. A shortfall of 340 aircraft by March 1938, and increasingly belligerent behaviour by Nazi Germany, demanded urgent attempts to redress the situation. The remedy required the ordering of large numbers of foreign-built aircraft, principally American, under conditions of the utmost secrecy. Consequently, by April 1938 the fighter aircraft needed (2303 in total) under Plan V had been revised as below:

1061 Morane Saulnier MS.405/406s

432 Bloch 151/152s

200 Curtiss Hawk 75s

120 Caudron-Renault 714s

200 Dewoitine D.520s

290 Potez 630/631 two-seat fighters

One of the major reasons for the chronic shortage of equipment in the *Armée de l'Air* was the fact that the new chief of the air force, the World War 1 fighter ace *Général* Joseph Vuillemin, was subordinate to the elderly *Général* Gamelin, Chief of the Defence Staff. Gamelin, as an army traditionalist, ensured that the army received the lion's share of the defence budget. Ominously, of even greater importance in the long term, his thoroughly conservative views on air power were not challenged by the lethargic Vuillemin.

The critical matter of co-operation between army and air force, which was so well developed by the Wehrmacht, and employed with devastating effect in 1940, was largely ignored. Indeed, the official French army Instruction gave the major role of attacking the enemy on the ground to the artillery – only troop concentrations were considered suitable targets for the air force. The Instruction further stated 'it is convenient to leave to the Air Force commanders the initiative for launching their attack'. It is hardly surprising that it proved virtually impossible to develop well co-ordinated counter-attacks against the Panzers in summer 1940.

In September 1938 came the Munich Crisis and the dismemberment of Czechoslovakia. The pace to war was accelerating. The question was could the French aviation industry provide the necessary equipment before the outbreak

This overhead view of Bloch 152C-1 No 8 gives a good impression of the nondescript appearance of the French camouflage. Just entering service in quantity in the spring of 1940, the Bloch proved to be a disappointment despite its heavy armament. The long barrels of the wing-mounted 20 mm cannon are clearly visible here

A close view of the immediate predecessor to the Bloch 152, the Bloch 151, which differed essentially in its Gnome Rhone 14N engine. Most of the 151s were relegated to training or point defence duties with the arrival of the improved Bloch fighter

of the war which was now clearly inevitable? Throughout the following months French aircraft production slowly gathered speed. It had already been recognised that the Morane Saulnier MS.406 – the most numerous *Armée de l'Air* fighter – was half a generation older than the later Bloch and Dewoitine types, even though it had once (briefly) been regarded as the best fighter in Europe.

A Bloch 152 of the *4eme Escadrille* (whose pennant emblem can be seen behind the canopy) of GC II/8 at Marignane in late 1940

The aircraft selected to replace it was the Dewoitine D.520, which was probably the finest French-designed fighter to see service in World War 2. With the best of intentions, but, with hindsight, possibly resulting in adverse effects upon the overriding need for fighters in quantity, orders were also placed for other replacement designs such as the Arsenal VG.33, Bloch 157 and C.A.O.200.

Frantic efforts were made to meet the requirements of Plan V (and its sub-developments), but years of neglect meant that while airframes were being turned out of the factories, there were critical shortages of components such as propellers and engines, which reduced the number of *'bon de guerre'* (combat-worthy) machines in the squadrons. A minor, but possibly significant, French practice in the light of subsequent events was the fact that squadron pilots had to collect new aircraft from the depots and factories themselves. There was no equivalent to the British Air Transport Auxiliary (ATA).

So it was that at dawn on 1 September 1939, the *Armée de l'Air* had accepted into its inventory a motley collection of types (totalling 1155 aircraft) made up as follows:

573 Morane Saulnier MS.405/406s

120 Bloch 151/152s

172 Curtiss Hawk 75s

7 Caudron-Renault 714s

0 Dewoitine 520

290 Potez 630/631 two-seat fighters

Looking for all the world like a model, this is Curtiss H-75A-1 Hawk s/n 37 (matricule militaire X-836). The first 41 aircraft delivered had only the four guns as seen here. The Hawks proved themselves to be the most effective fighters available to the French in the summer of 1940, with the majority of the top-scoring aces of this period flying the imported Curtiss type

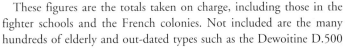

Sous Lt François Warnier in front of his Hawk at Suippes shortly before the Battle of France. Warnier scored eight confirmed and two probable victories between 20 September 1939 and 5 May 1940 while he was serving with GC I/5

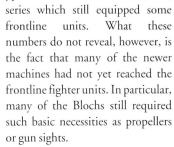

There were still many obsolete fighters such as the Dewoitine D.510, seen here behind *Sous Lt* Robert Thollon, in service in 1939. Thollon was one of the few aces to fly the Bloch 152, scoring eight confirmed victories while with GC I/8

These figures are the totals taken on charge, including those in the fighter schools and the French colonies. Not included are the many hundreds of elderly and out-dated types such as the Dewoitine D.500 series which still equipped some frontline units. What these numbers do not reveal, however, is the fact that many of the newer machines had not yet reached the frontline fighter units. In particular, many of the Blochs still required such basic necessities as propellers or gun sights.

The many shortcomings of the slowly resurgent *Armée de l'Air* were not lost on its personnel. Traditional French courage and élan were not lacking, indeed *Général* Vuillemin had declared that if war broke out he would wish to resign his position as Chief of Air Staff and die in a bomber over Berlin – in fact he was, to his credit, to serve as a lieutenant-colonel in a bomber unit in Tunisia in 1943.

The truth was that no amount of Gallic pride could, or would, make up for a lack of organisation and equipment in the time left before the German onslaught in the west began.

DROLE DE GUERRE

As the British declaration of war (issued some hours before that of the French) expired, the forward elements of the RAF's Advanced Air Striking Force (AASF) were already arriving at their new bases in France. The French air units began deploying to their satellite fields in the countryside, the Allied armies dispersed themselves along the frontier in line with their defensive strategies, and all waited for the Germans to make the first move. And waited.

Very quickly the opposing armies settled into the tedium of the *'Drôle de Guerre'*, or 'Phoney War', as the Germans concentrated on finishing off the Poles. In this phase of static warfare most of the air action for the fighters of the *Armée de l'Air* centred around border patrols and escorts for various reconnaissance aircraft in an uncanny echo of the tasks of the air services in the 1914-18 war.

On 8 September the first clash between the *Armée de l'Air* and the Luftwaffe took place near Landau when five Curtiss Hawks of GC II/4, which were escorting an observation aircraft, were attacked by four Messerschmitt Bf 109s. In the brief dogfight which followed, two of the German aircraft were claimed shot down by *Adjudant* Villey and *Sergent-Chef* Casenobe for the first victories of the *Armée de l'Air* in World War 2. Jean Casenobe would score five or six further victories before the Armistice in June 1940, and was eventually killed in an accident in North Africa in February 1943.

This type of operation set a daily pattern for the next few weeks as the opposing reconnaissance aircraft sought to establish what the enemy were doing, while the protecting fighters did their best to prevent them being shot down. On 20 September six Curtiss Hawks of GC II/5 were acting as fighter cover on such a mission in the Apach-Büdingen sector when the high flight was bounced by four Bf 109s of I./JG 53, led by the

Sgt Jean Gisclon in front of his Hawk at Toul in May 1940. The stork badge of SPA 167, the *4eme Escadrille* of GC II/5, is clearly visible. Position and size of the various *escadrille* badges varied widely

A pilot goes through the time-honoured pre-flight ritual while his crewchief warms up the engine of his Hawk 75. This particular machine (s/n 83) was reputedly photographed while serving with an advanced training unit (CIC) in the months prior to the campaign of 1940

The Hawk was a strong aircraft, with many surviving combat to end their days in training units. This machine is seen in 1943 over North Africa, but looks little different to those used in 1939-40

redoubtable Werner Mölders. Two Hawks were shot down in exchange for one Bf 109 destroyed and another damaged. The air war was beginning to increase in intensity.

On 24 September there were numerous inconclusive combats resulting in periodic losses on both sides until 1500 hours, when the six Hawks of GC II/4, which were escorting a Potez 637 of GR II/52 over the Eppenbrumm-Hornbach sector, met fifteen Bf 109s of I./ZG 52. *Sergent* de La Chapelle was shot down, and bailed out, but not before he had damaged one of his attackers. Two more were destroyed by *Adjudants* Dardaine and Camille Plubeau (the first of the 14 confirmed and 4 probables the latter pilot would score before the end of the French campaign). During the first month of the war, the *Armée de l'Air* had lost ten fighters in air combat (six Curtiss Hawks and four Morane Saulnier MS.406s) in exchange for claims of 20 Bf 109s destroyed.

The French tactical reconnaissance units had suffered rather worse. As the air combats increased in frequency and ferocity, the inadequacies of the antiquated French reconnaissance and observation machines became readily apparent, despite the best efforts of the fighters to protect them (19 had been lost by the end of the month). This, and the general timidity of the French High Command, led to the withdrawal of almost all such types from daylight operations to avoid further losses. Consequently, by October 1939 French reconnaissance efforts to determine German movements and intentions were virtually crippled.

Most air activity was curtailed by bad weather during October, and the fighters had little opportunity to add to their scores. Only four Henschel Hs 126 reconnaissance aircraft were claimed by the French for the entire month, the honours being shared equally between Hawks and Moranes. These types were more or less holding their own against the Messerschmitt Bf 109Ds of the Luftwaffe, but the need for more modern fighters was obvious. Taking stock of the situation, the French High Command decided upon a reorganisation of the *Aviation de Chasse* to take advantage of the arrival, it was hoped, of the Dewoitine D.520 in the early months of 1940.

Intended to be completed by May 1940, the plan called for the most urgent introduction of the D.520, Bloch 152 and, eventually, the Arsenal VG.33 into 15 *Groupes de Chasse* currently equipped with Dewoitine D.500/501s and MS.406s. Simultaneously, it was hoped to introduce progressive modifications to aircraft already in service in the form of variable-pitch propellers, armour plating and improved armament. The difficulties facing the groundcrews, who were already stretched coping with the many new problems presented by so many aircraft being introduced into service, can be imagined.

November began quietly enough, giving time to introduce a major change in the *Armée de l'Air's* tactical command system, whereby the overly complex *Escadres* used until then were replaced by *Zones d'Operations Aèriènnes*, with effect from the 21st of the month.

Hawk 75A-1 s/n 2 (matricule militaire X-801) '12' of *Sgt* Gisclon of GC II/5 at Reims immediately before the outbreak of war. It carries the emblem of SPA 167 on the rear fuselage and an unusually hard-edged camouflage pattern. The small 30 cm diameter upper wing roundels of the early war period can be seen on the wing of the machine in the foreground

Early afternoon on Sunday 6 November saw one of the fiercest (and in France one of the most celebrated) air combats yet when nine Hawks of GC II/5, escorting a Potez 63 of GR II/22 on a reconnaissance mission over the river Sarre, encountered a large formation of Bf 109Ds from I./ZG 2 at about 16,000 ft (see *Osprey Aircraft of the Aces 11 - Bf 109D/E Aces 1939-41* for further details). Led by Hannes Gentzen, the Luftwaffe's top-scorer in Poland, the Bf 109s were estimated at 27 strong – 20 were at the same altitude up-sun of the French, with the rest some 2000 ft higher. As the French turned into them the Germans attacked, and the engagement quickly broke up into a series of swirling individual combats.

Sergent Edouard Salès scored the first two of his seven confirmed victories when he chased one Bf 109 down to 500 ft where the pilot baled out, and then quickly followed this by hacking down another which crashed in a wood near the Sarre. Another future ace, *Sergent* André Legrand, claimed his second and third victories in this combat. The final claims were for five confirmed and five probables for the loss of *Lt* Pierre Houzé's aircraft which force-landed on the airfield at Toul, the pilot being unhurt, after a fight with Gentzen himself. In the event the claims were downgraded to four confirmed and four probables, possibly unfairly to the French pilots. That same evening Gentzen was summoned to Berlin for an explanation. The Hawks had clearly demonstrated their superiority over the Bf 109D, but increasing numbers of Bf 109Es were to make future combats far less one-sided.

German reconnaissance aircraft also suffered at the hands of the French pilots. Following on his success of the day before, Edouard Salès intercepted a Dornier Do 17P of 3.(F)/22 on 7 November south of Blieskastel. The machine crashed near St Ingbert with no survivors. On the 8th, ten Hawks of GC II/4, acting as escort to a French reconnaissance Potez, came across a Do 17P of 1.(F)/22, escorted by two Bf 109s. Upon sighting the French machines these turned away, abandoning the Dornier to its fate. Camille Plubeau raked it with fire, and the crew, one of whom was injured, baled out just prior to the aircraft blowing up.

The 8th also saw a MS.406 of GC III/2 downed when its pilot was separated from the rest of his formation, *Sergent* Barbey being wounded and taken prisoner. Two days later Hawk No 123 of GC II/5 was shot down by the rear gunner of a Do 17, *Adjudant* Dugoujon baling out uninjured.

Bad weather curtailed air activity until 21 November (the day the new *Zones d'Operations Aèriènnes* came into effect), when Edouard Salès became something of a specialist in downing Dorniers when he repeated his feat of the 7th of the month when, accompanied by *Lt* Tremolet, he attacked another Do 17P of 3.(F)/22 north of Morhange. This too crashed, two of the crew surviving to be made prisoner. That afternoon a *'patrouille lourd'* of six Hawks from GC II/4 bounced two Bf 109s of I./JG 52. The aircraft of the *Gruppenkommandeur*, Dietrich Graf von Pfiel, was sent down in flames by *Adjudant* Pierre Villey for his third victory. Villey scored one more confirmed and a probable before being killed in a mid-air collision on 25 May soon after shooting down his fifth confirmed victory. The second Bf 109 was shared by Jean Casenobe and *Sergent* Saillard.

The following day the French fighters again caught a Luftwaffe reconnaissance Do 17, this time from 4.(F)/121, which had its retreat cut off by four MS.406s of GC II/7 whilst returning from a mission. It was shot down in flames near Moos, in Germany. Three of the French pilots invovled, Georges Valentin, Gabriel Gauthier and Jacques Lamblin, were to become aces. The other pilot to share the victory was *Sous-Lt* Gruyelle. On this same day, as a direct result of earlier losses, the Luftwaffe instituted fighter sweeps in order to clear a path for their reconnaissance aircraft. Consequently, when a morning sweep by Bf 109s of 3./JG 2 surprised a patrol of Hawk 75s of GC II/4, *Sergent* Saillard was immediately shot down in flames and killed by Helmut Wick, while Camille Plubeau was lightly wounded in the leg and face in the vicinity of Zweibrüchen. His aircraft, No 169, was written off in the subsequent crash.

Again on 22 November (this time in the early afternoon), three linked formations of MS.406s from GC I/3, II/6 and III/7, escorting several reconnaissance machines over the French IV Army area, were attacked by Bf 109s from I./JG 76 and I./JG 51. In the ensuing fierce dogfights two German fighters from JG 76 were shot down (the pilots becoming prisoners) but one aircraft from GC II/6 and two from GC III/7 were also lost, one pilot being slightly injured. An incidental prize for the French was an undamaged Bf 109E which landed short of the German border when the pilot became disoriented during this fight.

On the 23rd of the month *Adj Chef* Pierre Le Gloan shared the first of

This unidentified MS.406 pilot (possibly *Cne* Raymond Clausse) of GC II/3 wears the cumbersome hard leather helmet used by French fighter pilots. Aircraft of the *4eme Escadrille* unusually wore code letters, as opposed to the numbers used by most other units

MS.406 s/n 451, (matricule militaire N-869) of *2eme Escadrille* of GC I/2 is seen early in 1940. *Adj* Dardaine was shot down in this aircraft on 15 May 1940, but the fighter was later repaired

his 19 victories (a Do 17P of 5.(F)/122) while flying an MS.406 with GC III/6.

Despite a lack of proper co-ordination with their RAF allies, French and British pilots occasionally fought alongside each other. Again on 23 November, a trio of Hurricanes from No 1 Sqn had intercepted a reconnaissance Heinkel He 111 near Verdun when they were suddenly joined by half a dozen Hawks from GC II/5. Such was the eagerness of the French pilots to get at the Heinkel that one Hawk collided with the tail of one of the Hurricanes, causing it to subse-

quently crash – fortunately with no damage to the pilot. The unlucky Heinkel was shared between all three RAF pilots and three of the French.

If November saw the French fighter pilots' greatest success so far, it also saw their worst losses until the German onslaught began in earnest in May 1940. By the end of November an H-75 and its pilot (*Lt Col* Robert Mioche) from GR 23 had been lost in combat, while two MS.406s from GC III/6 had been written off in collisions in bad weather, with both pilots killed. Two more MS.406s from GC II/7 caught fire in the air and were lost, both pilots suffering burns. One of these was *Sous Lt* Henri Grimaud who was to recover in time for the Battle of France, during which he downed five confirmed and three/four probables between 10 May and 15 June. Grimaud was later killed as a member of the Resistance when their base on the Vercors plateau was stormed by the Germans in 1944.

Some of the worst weather in living memory throughout most of December 1939 prevented much aerial activity. So restrictive was the weather that more pilots were lost in accidents than in combat, and only three victories were claimed.

A close-up view of the eagle emblem of SPA 75, the *2eme Escadrille* of GC I/5, on a Hawk

The main equipment of the French nightfighter and two-seat fighter units was the Potez 630. Its close similarity to the Bf 110, which caused so many recognition problems for both sides, is very apparent in this view. This is almost certainly the third production aircraft, matricule militaire C-515

INTO THE TORMENT

Following the occupation of Poland, the German forces in the west were gradually built up over the early months of 1940 ready for 'Fall Sichelschnitt', the mass attack on the Low Countries and France. Encounters between the French and German pilots began to occur more frequently, the first of the year being on 2 January when a dozen Hawks from GC II/5 shot down a Bf 109E of I./JG 53, although no claims were made by the French. The Moranes of GC II/7 were in action on the following day, claiming a Bf 109D for no loss. A week went by without operations because of the weather, then on the 10th a Bf 109 of I./JG 2 was claimed by *Sgt* André Legrand flying a Hawk from GC II/5 for his fourth victory. A day later the pilot who was to become the French 'aces of aces' during the Battle of France, *Lt* Edmond Marin La Meslée, accompanied by fellow GC I/5 pilot, *Sous Lt* Rey, caught a Do 17P of 3.(F)/11 at 22,000 ft above Verdun. The fire from their Hawks brought the Dornier down near the border, where the crew were captured. This was the first of Marin La Meslée's sixteen confirmed and four probables obtained during the battle for France. He was to die, as many other aces before him, while engaged in ground attack duties when his aircraft was struck by flak over Germany on 4 February 1945.

A notable victory was obtained on 13 January when a high-flying Do 17S-0 of 1.(F)/ObdL, flown by Lt Rosarius, was intercepted by *Cne* Barbier and *Sgt* Lemare of GC I/4. After a long chase down to sea level, the Dornier eventually crashed almost intact near Calais, the crew being captured. The aircraft's camera equipment proved to be of exceptional interest to the French. The kill was shared between the two pilots, and represented the first of 13 victories for Georges Lemare, including later actions with both the Vichy forces and with the *Normandie-Niémen* in Russia. Bad weather then again curtailed activity, with the result that only one more kill (a Bf 109E of 2./JG 54) was claimed (by *Lt* Gruyelle of GC II/7 flying an MS.406) before the end of the month.

Winter tightened its grip throughout February, with the result that not a single victory was scored, although three pilots were killed in accidents. March was little better; sporadic activity meaning that the only claims were for a Do 17 apiece for GC III/6 and GC II/7. Losses both in combat and accidents, however, continued to mount. An ominous portent was

Successor to the 'Lafayette' squadron of World War 1 fame was the *1ere Escadrille* of GC II/5. Here, Curtiss H-75A-2 s/n 140 (matricule militaire U-041) clearly displays the famous Sioux head emblem against a diagonal green band

Just entering service as the German attack began in May 1940, the D.520 was easily the best French fighter available. This is second prototype s/n 02, which is seen undergoing testing at the CEMA, at Villacoublay, in the summer of 1939. It differs most noticeably from production aircraft by virtue of the tailskid, lack of intake fairings to the super-charger on the engine cowling and the odd pitot head

An unidentified French fighter pilot shows off the equipment he wore while in the cockpit. Apart from the radio control box centrally placed on his chest, he also wears an oxygen regulator and mask, as well as a parachute and the rigid leather helmet. Compared to their RAF and Luftwaffe counterparts, the French pilots seemed to have been very cluttered with equipment

the loss of four MS.406s from GC III/7 in a single combat on the last day of the month, all of the pilots being killed or wounded. Three other aircraft were damaged. The victors were Bf 109Es of II./JG 53.

April opened to slowly improving weather and some brisk combats between the opposing sides. Two Moranes of GC II/2 caught a Do 17 of 4.(F)/11, which came down close to Sedan, while ten more MS.406s of GC I/2 engaged eight Bf 109s of II./JG 52 in their first serious combat of the war. In an inconclusive melée the Moranes claimed one Bf 109 damaged. Meanwhile five Hawks of GC I/5 trapped a Do 215 of 3.(F)/ObdL near Longwy, although the bomber made good its escape after slightly damaging one of its tormentors. In the early afternoon an He 111 was claimed by two MS.406s from GC II/2. No French fighters were lost.

On the following day a Bf 110 and a Do 215 were claimed by GC II/3, but a pilot from GC I/2 was killed when attempting to land his crippled aircraft. On the 4th came the shattering news of the German invasion of Norway and Denmark. A few quiet days followed, probably because the Luftwaffe was pre-occupied in Norway, and it was not until the 7th that the next encounter took place. In the morning MS.406s from both GC III/6 and III/2 attempted to catch a high-flying Do 17. As the fighters were only marginally faster, they were unable to do more than cause some damage, and it escaped. Soon afterwards a dozen Moranes from GC I/2 bounced six Bf 109s of I./JG 54 near Strasbourg. One was shot down by the 'Cicognes', but *Cne* Vidal was killed when his parachute caught on the tail of his aircraft after he baled out.

Later that day it was the turn of the French to be surprised when a formation of Moranes from GC III/3 were caught unawares by Bf 109s of II./JG 53. *Cne* Andre Richard was killed when he crash-landed. In the afternoon, I./ZG 2, newly-equipped with Bf 110Cs, met a mixed formation of Hawks and Moranes from GC I/5 and III/6 respectively. Two of the Messerschmitts were destroyed by the Hawks, but *Adj Chef* Salmand was killed in his H-75 by the gunfire of *Hpt* Hannes Gentzen. In the late afternoon some recompense for the French losses was obtained when a specially-equipped Ju 52 on a radio intelligence gathering operation was destroyed by Moranes from GC I/6 and II/7.

For the next few days the weather curtailed activities until 20 April when a notable event occurred in which a high-flying reconnaissance Ju 88 of 4.(F)/121 (which may have been already damaged) was caught by *Adj* Amouroux of GC II/9 and brought down as the first-ever victory for the Bloch 152. A vicious encounter between the Moranes of GC II/7 and Bf 109s of 2./JG 54 early the same day led to the first victory by Pierre Boillot, who exploded the aircraft of Lt Helmut Hoch with the fire from his 20 mm cannon. Later on a large formation of H-75s from GC II/4 were hit hard by Bf 109s from III./JG 53, one of the Hawks going down with a wounded pilot. The fighters of both sides were trying their hardest, but the reconnaissance machines and bombers they were trying to protect were being destroyed with depressing regularity. A solitary He 111 of KG 54 was chopped down near Maastricht by the combined efforts of several Morane pilots from GC II/3, including the later ace Martin Loï. This represented his first of his five confirmed victories.

Despite improving weather, there was little action for the French pilots until the end of the month, with only two Do 17s and a Bf 109 being

A line-up of some of the foremost aces of the Battle of France, all of whom were from GC I/5. They are, from left; *Sgt* Gérard Muselli (6 confirmed and 4 probable victories), *Sgt Chef* Léon Vuillemain (11 and 4), Czech pilot Sgt Frantisek Perina (11 and 2), *Lt* Edmond Marin La Meslée (16 and 4), *Cne* Jean Accart (12 and 4) and *Lt* Marcel Rouquette (10 and 4). Behind them is Accart's aircraft, which features the unit emblem of SPA 67

confirmed, one of the Dorniers being shared between the aces Edouard Salès and Pierre Villasecque and other pilots of GC II/5. During this time no fighters were lost in combat, although four (oddly, one of each of the four main types in service) crashed in accidents, all the pilots being killed.

Despite the accelerating French aircraft production programme, the *Groupes* were still desperately short of modern equipment. As the count-down to *Blitzkrieg* ticked away, there was still not a single frontline unit equipped with the D.520, although more Bloch 152 units were available.

The first nine days of May saw the Luftwaffe reserving its strength for the imminent offensive, although the French were kept busy chasing after the photo-reconnaissance Do 17s, He 111s and Ju 88s. In the calm before the storm, not a single kill was claimed, and the only loss was a pair of H-75s from GC II/5 (flown by the ace Edouard Salès and *Adj Chef* Delan-noy) which collided during an exercise, both pilots parachuting to safety.

A rare in-flight view of MS.406 s/n 546 (matricule militaire N-964) of the *5eme Escadrille* of GC III/6 seen returning from a mission in spring 1940. This angle reveals the intricate French camouflage. S/n 546 was damaged in a crash-landing on 4 May 1940

BLITZKRIEG

At 0535 on 10 May 1940, German forces launched one of the most significant military operations in history. By that date the fighters of the *Armée de l'Air* had scored 70 confirmed victories, the majority of them by the H-75-equipped GC II/4 and II/5. In so doing they had had 13 pilots killed and 15 wounded, and lost 28 fighters. The bomber and reconnaissance units had, however, fared far worse.

Utilising the experience gained in Poland and Norway, the Luftwaffe had expected to find the French, and their RAF allies, unprepared for the initial strikes. In this they were to be generally disappointed. Expecting trouble, the majority of the fields housing the fighter units had been active since first light, with patrols already in the air. At Suippes two Hawks of GC I/5 had been on such a flight since 0445. One aircraft had been forced back to base by engine trouble, but the other, flown by *Sgt Chef* François Morel, continued. Suddenly he met a formation of seven Bf 110s. Morel attacked and sent one down in flames, but he was immediately forced into a screaming dive to escape the rest of the pack. A friend of ace Jean Accart, Morel had already claimed a Do 17 in April, and by the time of his death in action on 18 May had accounted for ten aircraft confirmed and two probables. Whilst Morel was downing his Bf 110, Accart was also embroiled in combat with swarms of aircraft encountered soon after his dawn take-off (with Czech ace Frantisek Perina);

'Rising out of the shadows in a rapid climb, with no instructions from fighter control, I set course eastwards, where I could see a cluster of condensation trails lit up by the rising sun. With Perina a little lower down and astern, I climbed flat out towards them but was unable to reach them, so I set up a patrol in the Second Army's sector, between Sedan and Verdun. The sun was well up when I spotted 15 black dots, creeping westwards and to the south of our position. We headed for them, gaining altitude, for they were clearly higher than us. After a few minutes, we were close enough to identify them positively as Messerschmitt 110s.

'At that moment, they began a wide turn towards us. We were still a few hundred metres below them and I didn't think that they had seen us, because our aircraft camouflage would be blending in with the terrain below. They continued their gentle turn and I decided that they had not seen us, so I gave the order to attack. We were only two against fifteen, so there was time for only one quick pass, firing on the climb. I broke away as a group of five Messerschmitts turned towards me and I looked for Perina, but he was nowhere to be seen. I found out later that he had continued to fire in the climb for too long and had dropped away in a spin.

'Those twin-engined Messerschmitts were pretty manoeuvrable,

MS.406 no 777 (matricule militaire L-806) of Sgt Klebert Doublet of the *6eme Escadrille* of GC III/1. Doublet claimed six confirmed and one probable in this aircraft before being killed in a German attack on the airfield at Claye-Souilly on 11 June 1940

A Morane in a sorry condition. This is s/n 78, (matricule militaire N-393) of the *4eme Escadrille* of GC II/6, seen as it was left after a German attack on the airfield at Vertain on 16 May 1940. The 'Jeanne d'Arc' emblem of SPA 124 is clearly visible

Abandoned MS.406 s/n 1013 of EEA no 301. This aircraft almost certainly never reached the frontline before it was written off

but I got away by gaining altitude. The enemy formation seemed to have broken up in confusion, all except for a group of five which had formed up in line astern. I attacked this group head-on and fired on the leading aircraft, which was also firing at me. I passed underneath him and fired on each of the others in turn. It was all over in just a few seconds. The last one in line pulled up just as I opened fire and broke hard in case of a sudden attack from astern, but to my surprise the Messerschmitts regrouped and flew off to the east. I counted 12 and looked for the others. I couldn't see them against the glare of the sun, but I did see Perina climbing up to rejoin me.

'I was making my mind up whether or not to chase the Germans when I heard *Adjutant* Bouvard call over the radio to say that he was engaging a group of Dorniers near Reims, flying at 3000 metres. Bouvard, who was accompanied by *Sous Lt* Goupy, shot down one of the bombers, but then Goupy got an incendiary bullet in the thigh and just managed to make a forced landing at Wez-Thuisy before losing consciousness. Perina and I dived flat out towards the Dorniers, which were soon in sight, and attacked the bomber on the far left of the formation. He began to smoke, lost altitude and splashed himself all over a field near Suippes . . .

'Events unfolded at an infernal pace throughout the day. We had hardly been refuelled when we were ordered off to escort some Potez 63s which were carrying out a reconnaissance over the Ardennes. We passed over the enemy columns which were pushing westwards and had to dodge some severe flak . . . Back at Suippes we were placed on alert. Two hours went by, and I was just about to hand over to someone else when a flare shot up from the command post, ordering us to take off. Just as I got airborne, with Perina following, the airfield was carpeted with bomb-bursts. Looking up, I saw what seemed to be a mixture of Do 17s and Bf 110s, dead overhead at about 3000 metres.

'A furious battle developed. In the space of a few seconds I fired on a Dornier, went to the aid of a Curtiss that was being attacked by two Messerschmitts, and shot down a second Dornier just outside Suippes. Then, with Perina still clinging to me, I crept up behind a Dornier hidden under his tail, and fired a long burst into him, yawing a little so as to rake him from wingtip to wingtip. I was close enough to see the bullet strikes. I ceased firing and throttled back in order not to overshoot the target. The bomber's motors were still turning, but I saw one of the crew jump, his parachute opening as he swept past me. I pulled off to the right a little to watch the Dornier, and at the same time to keep an eye on some enemy fighters which were approaching.

'I saw a second crew member jump, but his parachute opened too soon and became snagged on the fuselage. I watched him struggling to free himself, trying to drag himself along the shroud lines towards the canopy. He pulled himself forward a little, then lost his grip and slid back towards the tail. The Dornier began to smoke, the pilot baled out and the bomber went into a vertical dive, dragging the trapped man with it. It impacted with a terrific explosion on the banks of a little river. I returned to Suippes with Perina as dusk was falling, after having destroyed another Dornier near Dun-sur-Meuse. So, for me, ended the first day of the battle.'

By the end of that day GC I/5 had been awarded eight confirmed victories over Do 17s. It was a different story on the field occupied by GC II/4, however. Thick fog had kept the pilots on the ground and they were unable to take-off before the Germans dropped some 50 bombs and destroyed six of GC II/4's Hawks. At Toul-Croix de Metz two pilots of GC II/5 managed to take off among a rain of bombs and pursue the Heinkels responsible for the damage, shooting down two. On their return they were reprimanded for taking off without permission, which may be why their victories were not confirmed until the day after. Meanwhile, the Moranes of GC III/1 at Norrent-Fontes had been warned trouble was on the way when an He 111 swept low over the field. The surviving fighters were hurriedly scrambled, and when a second group of Heinkels appeared the Moranes slaughtered six of them.

Another casualty was MS.406C-1 No 364 of *6e Escadrille* of GC III/3, abandoned at Vertain. The aircraft wore matricule militaire N-782 and a light blue diamond on the fin, along with a black '2'

A rare shot of two Bloch 152s of the *3eme Escadrille* of GC II/1 in flight in 1940. The Blochs had a mottle camouflage style all of their own, which was quite similar to that used on Italian aircraft, except for the colours

Unlucky '13' – an abandoned Bloch 152 which someone has clearly used for target practice

MS.406 s/n 1010 (matricule militaire L-600) also seems to have been abandoned at a repair depot. The use of a very light grey background to the camouflage, with darker patches carefully applied around the cockades, is similar to that seen on other aircraft previously in service with a fighter school, in this case the CIC at Montpellier

In the absence of any real air raid warning system, there were bound to be losses and the bomber fields suffered particularly heavily, but, at the end of the day the French fighter pilots had acquitted themselves well. In exchange for a dozen fighters destroyed (two pilots surviving wounded) they had destroyed 36 German aircraft.

There was now no doubt that the real time of trial for the French fighter pilots was at hand, and over the next few days they fought valiantly to stem the tide. The fighter pilots did their best to protect the bombers and reconnaissance aircraft in their charge, but hampered as they were by the indifferent quality of much of their equipment, and the tactics forced on them by an uncomprehending army staff, the scene was set for disaster. An example was the stupidity displayed by the army staff upon receiving news of the breakthrough at Sedan on 12 May. Despite photos, witnesses and the fact that the observer of the aircraft which discovered the German columns was a tank officer, the army command refused to believe the reports until the situation was irretrievable.

For the fighter pilots the next few days passed in a confusion of alerts and sorties. For the four Hawk *Groupes*, the main task was to provide air cover for the land armies. On 12 May five from GC I/5 caught a Stuka unit bombing French troops and swiftly decimated the dive-bombers. Eleven were shot down, three and a probable being awarded to Edmond Marin La Meslée alone. By 14 May GC II/4 had moved from its usual base at Xaffevilliers to Orconte, following a strafing attack by fighters which had cost it six aircraft destroyed on the ground. Only one pilot and aircraft had been lost in combat since the 10th, but the confusion of the move meant that only seven Hawks were serviceable by 15 May. Even so, the pilots of those seven gave a telling account of themselves when they met a formation of nine bombers, escorted by

Too many of the Moranes ended their days like this one. S/n 783 (matricule militaire L-812) served with GC III/1 until it was shot down on 26 May 1940, leaving its pilot with severe burns

This Bloch 152 was apparently abandoned while undergoing maintenance. Many otherwise serviceable aircraft had to be abandoned in the face of the rapid German advances in May-June 1940

half a dozen Bf 109s, at medium altitude over Reims. In a swirling dog fight, the French pilots, six of whom would later become aces, (Georges Baptizet, Camille Plubeau, Georges Tesseraud, Régis Guieu, Jean Paulhan and Jean Casenobe) brought down a Ju 88, four Bf 109s and an unlucky Hs 126 which blundered into the area. The seventh pilot, Vincotte, along with Plubeau, baled out due to battle damage, but not before the bombers had jettisoned their payloads far short of their intended target.

GC II/4's official diarist described the day's combat in the following entry;

'Wednesday, 15 May 1940. At dawn, while we were establishing ourselves in our new location, we were briefed to fly an air cover mission south-west of Charleroi. Take-off was fixed for 1100. All available aircraft were to take part; there were only seven. The pilots were selected from the 3rd and 4th *Escadrilles*: *Lt* Vincotte, *Sous Lt* Baptizet, *Sous Lt* Plubeau and *Adjudant* Tesseraud from the 4th, *Capitaine* Guieu, *Adjudant* Paulhan and *Sergent-Chef* Casenobe from the 3rd.

'We climbed without incident until we were over Reims, when we saw a superb V of nine twin-engined bombers heading south-west at 4000 metres. We decided to attack. They were escorted by half a dozen Messerschmitt 109s, 1000 metres higher up and a little behind. Lt Vincotte attacked, perhaps too soon. The Messerschmitts came down on us and we were forced to break away and dive for safety. Only Lt Vincotte stuck to the bombers and made several passes at the left-hand one (a Junkers 88). Meanwhile, Plubeau, Tesseraud and Baptizet were involved in a fierce dogfight with the 109s; each shot down an enemy fighter and then climbed rapidly to the aid of Vincotte. Together, they shot down one bomber; the remainder dropped their bombers haphazardly near Warmeriville and we went after them.

'Plubeau's cockpit was shattered by an explosive shell and he was forced to bale out. Vincotte damaged a second Junkers, then he too was hit in his fuel tanks and also had to bale out as his cockpit was filling with fumes and his oxygen equipment was out of action. Meanwhile, Baptizet, Guieu and Casenobe had spotted a Henschel 126 at low altitude, which they attacked and shot down in the forest of Silly l'Abbaye. In the process Guieu flew through a treetop at full throttle; by some miracle he managed to reach base and land safely with great gashes torn in his wings.'

While the Hawks generally managed to hold their own against greater odds, even if rather lightly armed, the pilots in the ten *Groupes* flying Moranes had more difficulty.

With a number of pneumatic systems which often failed after the slightest damage, guns which frequently froze-up and a performance not much better than many of the German bombers, it is surprising just how well they did. Again on 15 May, GC III/7 sent up a *'patrouille triple'* (nine aircraft) and were attacked by an entire *staffel* of Bf 109s over Mezières. With a 60 mph speed disadvantage, the Moranes quickly found themselves in a situation akin to a wagon train surrounded by Indians. Two soon went down in flames, followed by another three as more Messerschmitts arrived on the scene. Four Moranes eventually escaped, but the unit had lost two pilots killed, two injured and one missing. Despite this disaster, by the end of the day the French fighter arm had flown 254 sorties and had claimed 25 confirmed victories for the loss of 20 fighters.

Some pilots, however, found the Morane could bite, as shown by Robert Williame of GC I/2 who, on 5 June, shot down three Bf 109s in 15 seconds. Another ace who made good use of the Morane was *Sous Lt* Edouard Le Nigen of GC III/3, who claimed ten of his twelve confirmed kills in the MS.406 between 11 and 20 May. Tragically, he was to die of peritonitis in July.

As for the pilots of the nine *Groupes de Chasse* equipped with the Bloch 152 during May and June, every mission from which they returned was close to miraculous. Every unit flying the Bloch during May suffered severe losses, some purely as a result of the Bloch's lack of endurance – about 45 minutes at full throttle. In view of the type's shortcomings, the Bloch was mostly used as a bomber escort. It was not successful. *Groupement* 21, which included four Bloch units, had lost some 43 aircraft in combat by the end of May. Even worse, production of the fighter could barely keep pace with the losses. However, two pilots in particular proved that the formidable twin cannons of the Bloch could be put to good use. *Sous Lt* Robert Thollon of GC I/8, who scored eight kills on the type, wrote of his experience on 3 June;

'Our flight meets the Messerschmitts head-on. We break up into individual combats. Not seeing my wingmen, I wait to reassemble in the sector. Attacked from behind by a Messerschmitt which turns to the right

Great things were expected from the Arsenal VG.33 wooden fighters, but unfortunately, in an all too familiar story in France in 1940, not enough were delivered in time. These two aircraft were amongst a batch of twenty left undelivered at Villacoublay due to a lack of guns. They were subsequently captured intact by the Germans when they captured the airfield

with me following. The pilot does not bale out as the aircraft hits the ground. I am not able to check the point of impact as I am being attacked by more Messerschmitts, but *Caporal Chef* Spacek sees an aircraft fall between Roye and Chaulnes at about 0925. I am then pursued at tree-top height by two Messerschmitts for ten minutes, who make five attacks on me. At each attack I disengage to the right and then immediately left, finding myself every time in an excellent close firing position. In a moment only a single machine gun fires, then after two passes, no more. I return to base protected by the approaching defence flights.'

Thollon claimed all of his victories in less than six weeks. The other leading exponent of the Bloch was Louis Delfino, who scored six of his sixteen victories on the type.

By the end of that disastrous May, the *Groupes de Chasse* had destroyed 355 Luftwaffe aircraft for the loss of 163 of their own.

As if in acknowledgement of the parlous military situation, the beginning of June found most of France shrouded in fog and drizzle. This limited Luftwaffe operations considerably, allowing a sorely needed respite for the *Groupes de Chasse*. Since the end of May they had been in the throes of a major reorganisation to take account of the changing circumstances. This was completed very early on 3 June.

Although D.520 production was beginning to gain momentum, allowing the desperately needed re-equipment of some of the battered Morane units, other types were also being introduced. Among these were the Caudron C.714 lightweight fighter, which was issued to the Poles of GC I/145. A number of Polish pilots later fought with the RAF in the Battle of Britain (see *Osprey Aircraft of the Aces 21 - Polish Aces of World War 2* for further details). So grave was the situation that even the Dutch Koolhoven FK.58 was given trials.

Until June the *Armée de l'Air* had been more or less holding its own against the Luftwaffe in the air. Events on the ground, however, were conspiring to destroy its combat ability. The French army could, and on occasions did, offer fierce resistance to the invaders, but years of social discontent, a strong undercurrent of pacifism and incompetence at the highest political and military levels led to a rapid collapse in the morale of the troops, causing massive problems for the air force as the army began to disintegrate. They had no answer, any more than did the British and the other European nations, to *Blitzkrieg*.

Aircraft would take off only to find on return that the army units around them had retreated in panic, leaving the airfields unprotected.

Born out of the desperate need to supplement French fighter production, the Dutch Koolhoven FK.58 was ordered in small quantities. Some were issued to Polish-manned fighter units, but few, if any, saw actual combat

This in turn led to the abandonment of serviceable aircraft and the total disruption of the necessary support and maintenance services. In this situation the fighter pilots were being beaten on the ground. From 3 June they were going to find events in the air moving in the same direction.

Intelligence had indicated that the Luftwaffe was planning a massive attack on Paris, and its defending airfields, on 3 June along the lines of those on Warsaw and Rotterdam. All available units were deployed to meet this threat. At dawn on the 3rd there were some 60 aircraft on standby, including two-seat Potez 631s from the nightfighter units. In the oppressive heat all was quiet until lunchtime when suddenly three massive formations, totalling some 500 aircraft, were sighted en route for Paris.

The signal to take off arrived, but too late, with some units only receiving the message as the bombs were falling on their airfield. By the time the fighters reached the bombers, the latter were already turning for home and the greatly outnumbered French pilots found themselves fighting for their lives against the escorts. Yet this major effort by the Luftwaffe failed to achieve its objective. Very few French aircraft were destroyed on the ground and only 17 in air combat, (12 pilots killed) against an equal number of German aircraft lost in action during the course of the day.

This day was noteworthy as the day the Caudron 714 lightweight fighters made their combat debut. Flown by expatriate Poles, these little machines are officially credited with 12 victories, but suffered from technical problems and were found to be too fragile for combat.

On 4 June the evacuation from Dunkirk came to its conclusion. Despite this the *Armée de l'Air* was still fighting. On the following day, after a series of intense combats, the fighters claimed 55 victories for the loss of 15 fighters. There were many gallant actions during the course of that day; Henri Dietrich, flying the maligned Bloch 152, added two He 111s and a pair of Bf 109s to his score. and became the latest ace of GC II/10; Werner Mölders was shot down by René Pomier Leyrargues; and *Adj Chef* Pierre Dorcy, of GC II/2, made ace with the destruction of two

Another type of which much was hoped was the Bloch 700. Like the VG.33, it was primarily of wooden construction, and its light weight gave it excellent performance. The solitary prototype fell into German hands at Buc in mid-1940, however, and it was apparently destroyed by them soon after

Bf 109s. For the next five days the *pilotes de chasse* fought like men possessed, but forced to retreat from their bases in front of the advancing Germans, many aircraft had to be abandoned, and it became increasingly difficult to offer organised resistance – especially in the face of intense German flak. Even so, as more and more D.520s became available, the Luftwaffe was still being hurt, having lost 96 aircraft in air combat by 10 June. Six Ju 87s were brought down by GC I/2 on 8 June alone.

On 10 June Mussolini, expecting an easy victory, declared war on France. Several pilots scored or became aces on that day; *Cne* Marie Hubert Monraisse of GC II/5 brought down the fifth (a Do 17) of his seven confirmed kills; Louis Papin Labazordiere of GC II/7, his sixth and seventh, both Dorniers; and Charles Chesnais of GC II/9 his fifth and sixth, a Do 17 and an Hs 126. Altogether, the French pilots destroyed 12 aircraft that day, including three Bf 110s by GC I/5. Four days later the Germans entered Paris.

It was clear that things were not going to be as easy as the Italians had thought when Pierre Le Gloan brought down five Italian aircraft in a single sortie on the 15th, but the war situation was now irretrievable. It was another nine days before an armistice came into effect, to the utter dismay of the French fighter pilots who had fully expected to be battling on from North Africa. In that time only another ten German aircraft were destroyed, but four more fighter pilots were killed and two wounded.

Altogether, 138 French fighter pilots had been killed and another 176 wounded while defending their country by 24 June 1940. In the greater scheme of things, however, an almost unnoticed event had occurred on 18 June which would, one way or another, effect all the surviving pilots. From a BBC studio in London, an unknown army general named Charles de Gaulle announced 'the war is not lost'.

At the end of the Battle of France, the countryside was littered with the wrecks of French aircraft which had tried valiantly to halt the rout on the ground. This is a Breguet 693 light bomber, probably brought down by flak

Caught and destroyed on the ground by bombers that had overwhelmed the rapidly thinning ranks of the French fighter force , this Breguet 693 lies among piles of ordnance somewhere in France

TWO SIDES WITH THE SAME FLAG

Taking stock after the cease-fire, the French fighter force had lost 294 aircraft in air combat, 38 to flak and possibly another 100 destroyed on the ground. It is a sad irony that the *Armée de l'Air* was in fact stronger after the defeat, both quantitatively and qualitatively, than in September 1939. In July 1940 the seven best equipped (H-75 and D.520) fighter groups had retreated to North Africa, three more were in Syria, EC II/595 was alone in Indo-China and there were seven *Groupes de Chasse*, mostly equipped with Bloch 151 and 152s, and two nightfighter *Groupes* on the Potez 631, in France itself.

As early as 25 June 1940 the first three pilots, including Albert Littolf, had flown to join de Gaulle and create the embryonic Free French Air Force. Tragically, Gallic pride, still smarting from the recent defeat, turned many others against their erstwhile allies after the British attack on the French fleet at Mers el Kebir on 3 July. This led to the Germans allowing the new Vichy government to retain an air arm to be known as the *Armée de l'Air de l'Armistice*, to be based in the French colonies and the unoccupied zone of France. Consequently, some fighter pilots, obeying only the given word, fought for the wrong side until the demise of this air force in 1943.

DAKAR

Following the attack on Mers el Kebir by a reluctant Royal Navy, during which *Sgt* André Legrand, flying a Curtiss Hawk of GC II/5, shot down a Fleet Air Arm Blackburn Skua (the aircraft actually suffered no damage)

Seen soon after the Armistice, these Bloch 152s belong to the *3eme Escadrille* of GC II/9. Nearest is s/n 636, whilst just behind it is '71', which is believed to have been the mount of the commander of the unit, *Cne* Louis Delfino

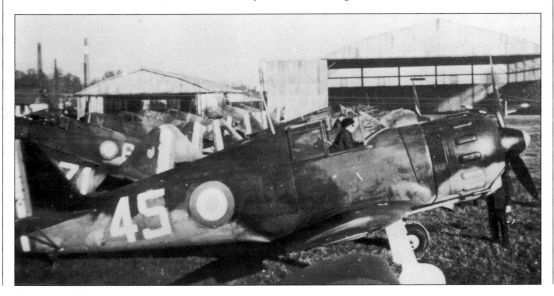

These Bloch 152s of *4eme Escadrille* of GC II/8, seen at Marignne in 1941, show off the distinctive fuselage numbers used by the unit.
It is worth noting that the Bloch-equipped units were all left in France when the *Armée de l'Air* began retreating to North Africa in 1940 in the hope of continuing the fight from there

Most of the home-based Vichy fighter units were equipped with the Bloch 152. These are from the *3eme Escadrille* of GC II/8 at Marignane in 1941

for his eighth confirmed victory, the Vichy government took immediate action to reinforce their overseas possessions. The stage was set for Frenchman to fight Frenchman.

Meanwhile, Dakar on the coast of French West Africa (Senegal), was seen as a potential threat to the Allies as the French battleship *Richelieu* was berthed there. On the other hand the port would be a valuable base for Royal Navy operations in the Atlantic if the authorities could be persuaded to join the Free French side. In September 1941 a large fleet was therefore assembled (including Free French vessels), which carried with it the 1st Fighter Group, manned by many of the first French airmen to join de Gaulle. Several of these later became aces with the Free French Air Force (FAFL), including Noël Castelain, James Denis and Albert Littolf. In the event, Operation *Menace,* as it was named, was a failure, and when the Free French emissaries failed to persuade their erstwhile colleagues to change sides, the Royal Navy took action.

The Vichy forces defended themselves vigorously, however, against a series of attacks by aircraft launched from HMS *Ark Royal* which began on 24 September. On that day *Sgt Chef* Georges Lemare of GC I/4 shot down a Swordfish for his fourth victory, and he went on to claim another nine confirmed with the *Normandie Niémen*. During three days of operations the Fleet Air Arm lost eight Swordfish, two Skuas and a Walrus to the aggressive French fighters, while several of the RN ships were damaged by gunfire from the *Richelieu* herself and bombing by *Aéronavale* Martin 167s. On 26 September the Royal Navy decided that there was little profit in pursuing the exercise and abandoned the operation.

SYRIA

Mandated to France since 1919, Syria and the Lebanon had long been a hotbed of intrigue and tension. After the Armistice of June 1940, the

authorities there rapidly decided to support the Vichy government. Large numbers of dissenters, including many Polish military escapees, then made their way to nearby British-controlled Palestine. Tensions were already running high between the various parties in the area when the Axis launched their attack on Greece and Yugoslavia in May 1941. This heightened fears amongst the Allies that the country might used as a base for operations against Egypt and the Suez Canal. When a rebellion threatened British interests in Iraq, the French in Syria both supplied arms to the rebels and allowed the Luftwaffe to use airfields there as staging posts to support the rebellion. In this situation, and provoked by the Free French, the British had no option but to take action. Consequently, strikes by the RAF were mounted on airfields in Syria. Although three weeks passed by with inconclusive skirmishes between Vichy French and British aircraft, the Vichy government in France was so alarmed by the continuous attacks that they sent in fighter reinforcements in the shape of 27 MS.406s of GC I/7 and 25 D.520s of GC III/6 from Algeria.

After the Iraqi insurgents suddenly capitulated on 31 May, it was decided by the British, who were again urged on by the Free French, to invade Syria before the Germans seized control. In fact, the latter had already lost interest in Syria, regarding it as a sideshow, and left it to the Vichy French, who were determined to resist any encroachment. Unaware of this, from 1 June the RAF began attacks on Syrian targets, leading to a bitterly contested campaign which was to last six weeks.

The first serious encounter took place on 8 June when Pierre Le Gloan, leading a *'patrouille double'* from GC III/6, met a reconnaissance Hurricane of No 208 Sqn over Damascus and shot it down for his 12th victory. Later that day, another six D.520s from GC III/6, led by *Cne* Léon Richard, met six RN Fulmars over the coast acting as CAP for a squadron of Royal Navy cruisers. Two of these were shot down, one by Richard for the first of his seven victories, all of which were British! On the following day, while protecting a bombing raid by the French on these same ships, Le Gloan downed two of the Hurricanes sent to intercept the bombers, but was unable to prevent the loss of two of the Bloch 200s. In the middle of this spirited dogfight three more D.520s, led by Léon Richard, and another three Hurricanes arrived. In the

Marin la Meslée is seen flying his Hawk s/n 217 over Rabat in Morocco in 1940-41. Apart from the white fuselage line, there is little to distinguish the Vichy finish from the ill-fated French campaign of 1940

Another line-up of aircraft from GC II/8, this time taken in 1942. All wear the red and yellow 'Vichy' stripes on the tail and cowling. Number 14 is a Bloch 155, s/n 708, limited production of which continued after the occupation

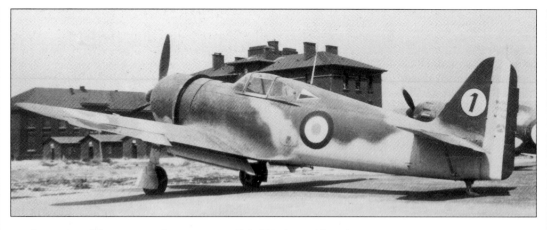

confusion, one of the D.520s and a Hurricane collided head-on, although both pilots were rescued from the sea by the Royal Navy.

As French resistance on the ground stiffened, both sides sent in air reinforcements. On the French side these consisted of ten D.520s from GC I/2 and four MS.406s from a training school. Both sides undertook numerous bombing raids on the other's ground forces over the next few days, and losses to the French bombers, in particular, were very serious, due both to accidents and enemy action. The French fighters were having more luck, however, for on the 13th Léon Richard shot down a Blenheim from No 11 Sqn, killing its entire crew.

At the end of the first week's fighting the action on the ground was almost at a stalemate, but while the RAF had much the same strength as it had started with, the French sent in yet more reinforcements. These included 21 D.520s of GC II/3.

On 15 June six D.520s, led by Le Gloan, caught six Gladiators by surprise, one of the biplanes being immediately shot down by the ace for his 15th confirmed kill. In a confused engagement one of the D.520s was also destroyed and another of the Gladiators severely damaged, as was Le Gloan's aircraft, forcing him to crash-land back at his base.

A better overall view of a Bloch 155, in this instance s/n 707 of the *4eme Escadrille* of GC II/8. This is the personal machine of the commanding officer, *Cne* de Vaublanc

Most of the Bloch 155s were seized by the Germans and used as advanced trainers when the whole of France was eventually occupied in late 1942

Armourers are seen working on a Bloch 152 of GC II/8 at Marignane in 1942. A shark emblem of the *3eme Escadrille* can be just made out below the radio antenna. The machine wears full Vichy stripes and, surprisingly, still retains its matricule militaire

In a series of encounters between the two sides over the next few days, it was the bombers that suffered most, but the serviceability of the French fighters was also declining rapidly. On the ground fierce fighting was continuing, but a temporary stalemate in the Western Desert allowed the British to send in more reinforcements.

By 22 June – the day the German invaded the USSR – it was apparent that the influence of the Free French was beginning to effect the morale of the Vichy forces.

On the following day, the arrival of RAF reinforcements allowed a change of tactics. A series of strafing attacks on the French airfields commenced. After an initial interception of bombers at Baalbeck, the D.520s of GC III/6, again led by Le Gloan, were scrambled and soon encountered eight Hurricanes. In a vicious exchange four of these were claimed shot down, one by Le Gloan and another shared between *Cne* Richard, *Sgt Chef* Mertzisen and *Sgt* Coisneau. A third was brought down by *Lt* Marcel Steunou, who shared in a fourth with two other pilots. These two victories, plus a Fleet Air Arm Fulmar downed over Saida on 8 June and two German aircraft in France in 1940, made Steunou an ace. He did not get to enjoy his status for long, however, for later that same day both he and *Sgt* Savinelin were killed during an engagement with a dozen Australian Tomahawks from No 3 Sqn. Even though Léon Richard destroyed one of the Tomahawks to thus become

The rudimentary design of the MS.406 is clearly apparent in the poor fitting panels on the engine of this machine, in service with the Vichy training school at Aulnat

an ace, the remaining aircraft of GC III/6 were all roughly handled by the Australians, with Le Gloan's aircraft being seriously damaged.

On 26 June, the aggressive Australians caught the D.520s of GC II/3 on the ground at Homs and destroyed five, seriously damaged six more and shot up another eleven to varying degrees. The situation for the French airmen was depressingly similar to that which had existed in France a year earlier, when the absence of an early warning system meant that the fighters were often taking off as bombs were falling on their field.

The disaster for the French at Homs led to the withdrawal of all French fighter units to await replacements. For the rest of the campaign, French fighter strength was effectively broken, even though they were to exact a cost from both the RAF and RAAF before the end. The French bombers meanwhile (many from the *Aéronavale*), were to continue to suffer much as they had back in 1940.

On 2 July *Sous Lt* Emile Leblanc of GC II/3 claimed a Hurricane (not in fact lost) to add to the six confirmed and one probable German

Another French-based unit to use the Bloch 152 was GC I/1, whose aircraft are seen here at Lyon-Bron in 1942. The nearest aircraft, s/n 606, carries the cockerel badge of SPA 48, adopted by the *2eme Escadrille*

Photographed almost certainly in Morocco in late 1940, this D.520 belongs to an unidentified unit. The fighter wears the early Vichy fuselage stripe

D.520 '11' of GC III/6 is seen in flight towards the end of 1940. The aircraft's pilot remains unidentified

D.520 s/n 248 is seen on patrol somewhere over North Africa at the end of 1940. The panther badge denotes that the aircraft belongs to the *2eme Escadrille* of GC II/7

machines he had destroyed over France. Ironically, he was killed while piloting a Hurricane when he accidentally collided with a P-39 during a training flight on 29 January 1944. Later, on 5 July, six D.520s of GC III/6 (as usual led by Le Gloan) shot down two Hurricanes, the kills being shared between Le Gloan, Mertzisen, Richard and *Sgt Chef* Martin Loï. Loï was another French pilot to become an ace at the expense of the RAF, this being his fifth confirmed kill to add to four claimed earlier with GC II/3 in France. He was killed on 27 July 1943 when he was forced to abandon his Airacobra during a training flight. He baled out but his parachute caught on the aircraft and he was dragged to his death.

Of interest during this campaign is the use of the MS.406 as a makeshift nightfighter, when GC I/7 attempted to use them against RAF bombers. Surprisingly, *Adj Chef* Amarger succeeded in bringing down a Wellington of 70 Sqn on 7 July.

Heavy fighting was continuing on the ground, but the end was close. Both sides carried out strafing attacks on their opponent's airfields, but the French were now beginning to cut their losses and withdraw their aircraft. On 12 July 1941 all fighting ceased, and Syria passed into Free French control.

The Vichy forces had lost 128 aircraft from all causes, but only nine fighters in air combat. They had claimed 34 confirmed kills in the air (RAF/RAAF losses actually 27). Their opponents claimed 37, against an actual loss of 26. Honours were therefore about even. The focus of the action was now about to move back to North Africa.

Pierre Le Gloan is seen at the controls of his famous D.520 (s/n 277) '6', painted in full summer 1940 Armistice markings

OPERATION *TORCH*

After the stunning Axis victories in the USSR in mid-1942, there was an urgent need both to relieve the pressure on the Soviets and save Egypt. The Allies finally decided upon a landing in French North Africa which would both open a second front, and present the opportunity to finally defeat the Italo-German forces in North Africa. This would thereby expose the German's southern flank, as the Mediterranean would be once more under Allied control. Named Operation *Torch*, it was the first major Anglo-American military operation, and in the hope of lessening local Vichy resistance, was strongly touted as being a mainly US and Free French affair.

The need to occupy as much ground as possible before the Axis could respond led to the decision to land simultaneously in three widely separated locations. These were to be at Casablanca, Oran and Algiers, the former being the exclusive responsibility of the Americans, whilst joint US/British forces would seize the the latter two cities. A disadvantage for the Allies was that the trio of objectives diluted the available forces, but they had little choice in the matter.

Three separate convoys were required, each with several aircraft carriers whose aircraft were to cover the initial landings. Force 'H' to Algiers was British, and included four carriers with a total of 118 aircraft; Force

Sgt Georges Lemare, of *2e Escadrille* of GC I/4, was photographed in his H-75A-3 No 295 on patrol from Cap-Vert, near Dakar. His aircraft wears full Vichy markings from the 1942 period. At this time he had five victories to his name, and the rest of his tally would be amassed whilst flying with the *Normandie-Niémen* in Russia

'O' to Oran (Algeria) used three Royal Navy carriers with 59 aircraft; while the US Navy supplied four carriers for the Casablanca (Morocco) landings, which had 164 naval aircraft, plus the P-40s of a USAAF fighter group. Utmost secrecy was required, especially as the American force was sailing directly across the Atlantic. Additional air support was also to be available from forces specially sent to Gibraltar and Malta.

To oppose these aerial armadas the Vichy French had 205 aircraft in Morocco, of which 78 were fighters (38 D.520s and 40 H-75s), shared between GC I/5, GC II/5 and *Aéronavale Flotille* 3F. In Algeria there were 160 aircraft, including 76 fighters – mostly D.520s with GC II/3, GC III/3 (this unit had been previously numbered GC I/3, and returned to that designation on 8 November) and GC III/6. The Tunisian forces were the weakest with only 69 aircraft, including 24 D.520s of GC II/7.

Surprise was complete when all three landings began at 0100 on 8 December 1942. The first dawn strikes at La Sénia airfield, near Oran, by RN Albacores were intercepted by a dozen Dewoitines of GC III/3 from the base, and in a swirling combat near the target, the D.520s claimed four shot down and two probables before they were set upon by the escorting Sea Hurricanes. Two of the bombers were claimed by *Lt* Georges Blanck, who had already scored six confirmed Luftwaffe kills with GC I/3 in France. Four D.520s were shot down in return.

An attack at Tafaroui by Seafires of No 807 Sqn caught several bombers on the ground, and while returning, the fighters intervened in the fight with GC III/3 described earlier, and claimed a D.520 as the first ever victory for the Seafire. No 807 Sqn also destroyed several aircraft on the ground at La Sénia for good measure. In return, ground fire shot one of the Seafires down.

At about 0800 Sea Hurricanes of No 891 Sqn attacked La Sénia. Having exhausted their ammunition, one was shot down, probably by Sous Lt Michel Madon for his eighth victory – the pilot was unhurt.

It had been intended that US paratroops, flown directly from England, should have been landed at La Sénia, but the formation of US C-47s carrying them got lost and dispersed in bad weather. Arriving just after the

Two Hawks of GC I/5 on patrol somewhere over Morocco in early 1942

attack by the No 807 Sqn Seafires, they were intercepted by the D.520s of GC III/3, which were still in the air, and a dozen were forced down in a salt lake some distance away and then strafed by the Frenchmen. Soon afterwards it was discovered that Tafaroui was now in American hands, and the C-47s were instructed to take off again and divert to there. Those that could did, but some had bogged in and were unable to do so.

Later that hectic morning, the Dewoitines of GC III/3 were orbiting over La Sénia prior to undertaking a bomber escort mission when a formation of fighters, which they took to be Hurricanes, appeared. They were actually Seafires from No 807 Sqn, and in the affray which followed, one was downed by *Sgt* Poupart in exchange for D.520.

In mid-afternoon GC III/3 met yet more Seafires of from No 807 Sqn over La Sénia. Returning after an uneventful bomber mission in which no bombs were actually dropped, a *'patrouille double'*, led by *Cne* Roger Duval, caught the British fighters attacking aircraft on the ground. In a brief engagement one was shot down by Duval for his fourth victory.

Two of the MS.406s which formed part of Free French Flight No 2 in Rayak in Syria in late 1941. Nearest to the camera is s/n 831

Later still that day the busy GC III/3 were strafing the airfield at Tafaroui (by then in American hands) when the US 31st Fighter Group arrived direct from Gibraltar. Flying Spitfires, the Americans at first mistook the D.520s for Hurricanes, and in the confusion, *Sous Lt* Georges

Pissotte shot one of the Spitfires down for his fourth confirmed victory. As soon as the Americans realised their mistake, however, they turned on the D.520s. In an unequal fight, *Cdt* Engler and *Cne* Mauvier never had a chance, both being killed, whilst *Sgt* Pouparte took to his parachute.

On their way back to base the six surviving members of GC III/3 came across the unlucky C-47s, which had landed earlier and were unable to take off. These were comprehensively strafed and three were destroyed and awarded jointly to Georges Blanck, *Sous Lt* Michel Madon, *Sous Lt* Georges Pissotte and Roger Duval. All four were already aces and, after 8 November, their next claims would once again be against the Germans. For Madon these were his 9th-11th victories. His eighth had come earlier that day when he brought down a Sea Hurricane of No 891 Sqn. Blanck's final kill was against an Me 323 transport near Bastia on 30 September 1943. He finished the war in command of a fighter training school in Meknes, Morocco. Postwar, he saw action in Algeria again and retired as a colonel in October 1963. He died on 8 January 1990. As for Pissotte, he claimed an Me 323 confirmed and a Do 217 damaged in September 1943 to give him a final score of eight confirmed and a probable. After the war he served for 18 months in Indo-China, before returning to various training posts and retiring as a colonel in 1964. For Duval the C-47s gave

him seven confirmed victories. His next claims comprised a Ju 52 confirmed, three damaged and a probable all on 29 September 1943 off Bastia (Corsica) to give him a final tally of eight confirmed and two probables. Duval's postwar career saw mostly involved in training and staff posts. He retired as a general in July 1961.

As for GC III/3, it was with immediate effect renumbered GC

MS.406 s/n 819 (matricule militaire L-848), previously of GC I/7, was used by Jean Tulasne to escape to Palestine from Vivhy-controlled Syria on 5 December 1940. It is seen here in FAFL markings when it formed part of the new GC 1 'Alsace'

This is MS.406 s/n 819 again, but now masquerading in RAF markings as AX619

I/3, being officially credited with 17 confirmed and 7 probable victories while part of the Vichy forces.

After only one day the air fighting around Oran was effectively over, and the surviving aircraft began withdrawing to Morocco. Resistance on the ground continued for another two days – long enough to save Gallic face – before *Admiral* Darlan, commanding all Vichy forces in North Africa, and previously a staunch supporter, changed sides and ordered a cease-fire. The RN had lost a staggering total of 53 aircraft of all types, although most of these were put down to insufficient pilot training.

Over in Morocco the story was rather different. Initially, the defenders were confused and the American troops came ashore very quickly, but their inexperience kept them on the beaches too long, giving the French time to rally. At dawn US Navy aircraft attacked ships in the harbour and carried out strikes on the airfields, catching aircraft taking off and causing great execution. As the Grumman F4Fs swept in over Casablanca, six Hawks of GC II/5 'Lafayette' were taking off from Camp Cazes. Among the pilots were numerous aces from the fighting in 1940. One of the first away was *Lt* Pierre Villaceque, who already had five confirmed kills against the Germans. His patrol scored first blood when they downed an OS2U observation float-plane and disrupted the gunfire from the USN ships offshore.

At regular intervals more aircraft of GC II/5 took off to maintain standing patrols. At 0845, even though suffering from sciatica, *Cdt* Tricaud lifted off, accompanied by *Lt* Fabre and *Cne* Robert Huvet. A member of the *Aéronautique Militaire* since 1930, the highly experienced Huvet had downed five

D.520 no 309 of the *5eme Escadrille* of GC III/6 at Tunis in May 1941. It had been intended that this aircraft should reinforce the Vichy elements in Syria, but *Sgt Chef* Ravily damaged it in transit while landing at Catania, in Sicily. It was not returned by the Italians until 29 March 1942

The yellow tail applied to the D.520s used in Syria is clearly visible on no 229 of GC III/6. This was the aircraft flown by the commanding officer of the *5eme Escadrille, Cne* Jacobi. It was photographed almost certainly at Brindisi on 25 May 1941 while the unit was on its way to Syria

This crash-landed D.520 of GC I/2 gives a clear view of the red and yellow Vichy markings, modified with an interesting sweep to the rear of the horizontal stripes on the cowling. The stork insignia is that of SPA 103

German aircraft in France and probably an RAF Wellington off Safi on 2 September 1942. Today he was going to shoot down Americans. Another of the Hawks responding to the invasion was flown by *Lt* Paul Abrioux, who was normally stationed at the HQ in Rabat. Joining in the action regardless, events on 8 November were to make him an ace.

As the last of the tired old Hawks struggled for airspeed, the Wildcats of VF-41 began a high-speed pass across the airfield. They were engaged at that precise moment by the Hawks. Although GC II/5 had 13 D.520s on strength, and the American pilots reported seeing them, in fact not a single one was used as the unit had no ammunition for its 20 mm guns. In a vicious and confused dogfight which raged over the field, the greater firepower of the Wildcats was telling. Five French pilots were killed in combat, four were wounded and two more killed in take-off accidents.

Apart from aircraft lost in combat, GC II/5 had others destroyed on the ground, a total of 13 being lost in all. Among the dead were Tricaud and Robert Huvet, but not before each had shot down an F4F. Pierre Villaceque was credited with one of the American fighters for his sixth confirmed kill to add to his two probables, but was wounded in the face. He later saw service in Tunisia and Italy, before being promoted to command GC I/3 until the end of the war. Postwar, he took on increasingly important staff and planning roles. In 1962 he was made a general, assuming the post of personnel director for the *Armée de l'Air* in 1969. He retired in 1977. Paul Abrioux claimed his fifth and final victory that day (an SBD Dauntless), and remained in North Africa postwar. After serving with the UN in Palestine in 1948, he joined the French Air Ministry, but was killed on 17 November 1951 when he was forced to abandon the P-47 Thunderbolt he was flying and his parachute failed to open.

As for the US forces, they too had paid a price – in total, GC II/5 claimed seven Wildcats and an OS2U for the day, although some of the fighters may actually have been SBDs. The French were not alone in misidentifying their victims. In an episode that typifies the poor general level of aircraft recognition at the time, that same morning the inexperienced American pilots of VF-9 shot down a twin-engined aircraft which they claimed was a LeO 45 off Fédala – in fact it was an RAF Hudson. The mistake was compounded the following day when VF-41 shot down an

This Curtiss Hawk of the *1ere Escadrille* of GC I/5 is seen at Rabat, in Morocco, in 1940. The number '1' probably indicates it is the CO's aircraft

unarmed RAF PR Spitfire. All in all, it was not a good day for the pilots of VF-9, who lost six of their aircraft due to mechanical failures and bad navigation, without any help from the French.

As Monday 9 November dawned over Casablanca, five weary pilots of GC II/5 strafed landing craft at Fédala, and were lucky to escape with only minor damage. The Americans responded by sending up standing patrols of Wildcats to cover the fleet. An hour later, a similar attack by a mixed formation of *Armée de l'Air* and *Aéronavale* bombers, escorted by 15 Hawks from GC I/5, was spotted by the pilots of VF-9. With the advantage of altitude, the Wildcats rapidly knocked down four of the Hawks, killing two of the pilots and gravely wounding *Adj Chef* Georges Tesseraud. Th latter was a highly capable pilot, having claimed seven confirmed and four probables in France, most of them Bf 109s. Fortunately, he recovered in time to shoot down a Ju 88 off Oran on 11 April 1944. After the war he had two tours in Indo-China, interspersed with a stay in Morocco. He retired in 1964 as a colonel and died on 29 July 1988.

Lt Camille Plubeau, one of the best pilots on either side that day, with 14 confirmed kills and four probables (all from the French campaign), was luckier. His aircraft was badly damaged and he had to make a wheels-up landing back at his base at Rabat, but was uninjured.

The only consolation for the French was when yet another GC I/5 ace, *Sgt Chef* Jérémie Bressieux, claimed the only Wildcat of the day when he downed Ens Gerhardt (who was unhurt) for his ninth, and last, confirmed victory of the war. A year later he was flying a P-39 *with* the Americans. Postwar, he served mostly as an instructor until 1954 when he

These two Hawks are from GC II/4, and were photographed in flight over Morocco sometime in 1940-41. The large fuselage numbers are the 'last two' of the aircrafts' serial – i.e. 188 and 267. Both carry the 'Petit Poucet' emblem of SPA 155

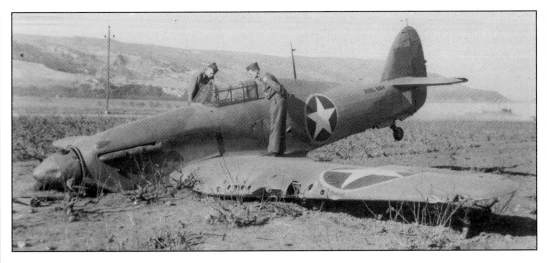

The Fleet Air Arm had a hard time during *Torch*, suffering a number of casualties at the hands of the Vichy French fighter force. Sea Hurricane JS327 of No 804 Sqn was amongst the aircraft shot down, the fighter being force-landed on a beach at Les Andalouses, near Oran in Algeria, on 8 November 1942 after combat with French D.520s. The unit flew from HMS *Dasher* during the *Torch* landings. Note the 'Americanised' roundels, which were employed to aid identification during the operation

American GIs examine derelict Hawk 75s of GC II/5 at Medouina shortly after the end of Operation *Torch*

went to Indo-China. He returned to France in 1956 and retired as a lieutenant-colonel in 1961.

While the pilots of GC I/5 were fighting for their lives over Fédala, the Americans attacked bases across a wide front, destroying many aircraft on the ground. And although it was now impossible for the French airmen to mount any kind of operations, on the ground, resistance was still strong.

By 10 November most of the surviving French air units had withdrawn to Meknes. With the fighters effectively pinned to the ground, the American aircraft were able to attack the Vichy ground forces virtually unmolested. Early on the morning of the 11th, *Général* Nogues, the Vichy army commander, sued for a cease-fire, thus bringing the fighting to a close. On Friday 13 November final agreement was reached between all parties, and the French in Africa were all once more on the same side, and the *Armée de l'Air de l'Armistice* ceased to exist.

Any illusions that the remaining supporters of Vichy may have had about the true nature of their relationship with the Germans was swept away when that same morning the Wehrmacht extended its occupation to the whole of France.

WITH THE RAF

After the disaster of June 1940, those courageous French troops who first responded to the appeal of de Gaulle, or simply made up their minds to fight on regardless, made their escape to England by any number of daring adventures. Notable among these is *Lt* Pinot, who determined to bring the entire training school he then commanded in Brittany. On 18 June 1940 he commandeered a fishing boat and brought 108 trainees, and the padre, to England. Others came alone, some via Spain or farther afield – a few, such as Albert Littolf, brought their aircraft with them. On 1 July 1940 this ragtag of mostly junior ranks was named the *Forces Aériennes Françaises Libres* (FAFL). At first, however, there were so few airmen that they were put under the command of the French navy, with *Amiral* Muselier at their head. It was Muselier who gave the FAFL their most famous emblem, the Cross of Lorraine.

At first Muselier was assisted by the nucleus of an Air Staff, made up entirely of reserve officers. In February 1941 *Lt Col* Pijeaud arrived from French Equatorial Africa and was made Chief of Staff of the FAFL. He died of wounds received in action in North Africa in January 1942.

Unlike the citizens of all other occupied countries, whose legitimate governments fled to England and supported their expatriates in their resistance, the French were strongly discouraged from joining the Allied camp. Indeed, many served for years in the FAFL with a Vichy sentence of death hanging over them. As a consequence many pilots operated with a false name to protect both themselves and their families back in France.

A transit camp was formed at Odiham in June 1940, and it quickly became apparent that the impatience of the French to get into combat, and the radically different training methods of the RAF, were resulting in a high accident rate. Nevertheless, a few French pilots served in the Battle of Britain, and as early as August 1940 the first bomber unit of the FAFL was formed at Odiham. As an aside, it could be argued that the French had already played their part in the Battle by weakening the Luftwaffe.

A number of French pilots also served as members of RAF units. The most famous among these is indisputably Pierre Clostermann. Officially credited by the *Armée de l'Air* with 33 victories (recent British sources give him about 15) to make him their 'ace of aces', Clostermann scored his

Clipped-wing Spitfire LF IXs of an unidentified French unit, photographed almost certainly in Italy or Corsica in 1944

first kills with No 341 Sqn, but the majority appear to have been claimed with No 602 Sqn. Postwar, he described his exploits in the *The Big Show.*

The rollcall of French pilots in the RAF also included James Denis, who had made a daring escape from France in a Farman 222 with 19 others in June 1940. Although then 34 years old, having learnt to fly in 1929, Denis thought he had missed his chance for combat. Briefed by de Gaulle himself to rally support in Cameroon, he then found his way to Egypt, then Greece and eventually the Western Desert, where he was attached to No 73 Sqn. With them, in one month of combat (May 1941) over Tobruk, he downed nine aircraft, all confirmed. One, a Bf 109E which crash-landed on 23 April, was flown by Ofw Hans-Joachim Marseille . . .

Denis then went to Syria, where his diplomatic skills helped prevent French airmen fighting each other, before returning to join the FAFL HQ. Postwar, he commanded the base at Bourget before retiring in 1953.

Many of the first French pilots in the RAF proved to be exceptional. Jean-Francois Demozay, better known by his *nom de guerre* 'Morlaix', was discharged soon after call-up in 1938 as being unfit for military service. A civil pilot, at the outbreak of war he served as an interpreter with the RAF. After the collapse, and discovering an abandoned Bristol Bombay in June 1940, he flew this, along with 15 troops, to England. Claiming to be a fighter pilot, he joined the FAFL, then No 1 Sqn RAF, and proved to be precisely that. A report of his activities on 9 August 1941 read, 'A magnificent example of courage and skill. On 12 July, descending to low level he attacked and destroyed an enemy aircraft over northern France. On 17 July he sank enemy mines with his cannon. On the 26th he shot down his seventh enemy aircraft. 31 July, off Dunkirk, he engaged three Bf 109s in combat. He shot down two and damaged the third for his eighth and ninth kills'. Sadly, after service in FAFL HQ and in France after D-Day, he was killed in a flying accident near Buc on 19 December 1945. At the time of his death he had 21 officially confirmed kills and two probables, most while with No 91 Sqn. Not one was shared.

When it came time to form the first French fighter units, it was decided that they would have their own national character, but would be integrated into the RAF, despite the misgivings of many who would have preferred to create a new national air force. Consequently, the 1st Fighter Group, commanded by *Lt Col* Lionel de Marmier (who had earlier been involved with the Polish-manned GC I/145) was organised. It had four flights as follows: 1st (Fighters), with two D.520s; 2nd (Bombers) with six Blenheims; and 3rd and 4th (Reconnaissance) with six Lysanders each, and a pair of Caudron Lucioles for liaison. The unit took part in the unsuccessful expedition to Dakar, where the Lucioles were lost.

Simultaneously with the creation of the FAFL in Britain, a few French airmen had found their way to Egypt from Syria. Formed into Free French Flights 1, 2 and 3, they were equipped with a miscellaneous selection of aircraft, many French, and a few Hurricanes. They fought well in the early desert battles of 1941, but had been wiped out by June of that year, and surviving pilots were incorporated into the RAF. Probably the most famous of these was Albert Littolf who, on 5 May 1941, downed four Bf 109s over Tobruk to take his score to ten confirmed. Additionally, there were a few detachments in the other Free French African territories.

It was with the arrival of *Lt Col* Martial Valin in England that the FAFL

Cdt Henri Hugo, an ace with six confirmed and two probable kills, is seen leaving the cockpit of his Spitfire at Ajaccio in late 1943. All his victories had been claimed in the 1940 campaign in France while he was with GC II/7, flying the MS.406. Note the unit badge aft of the cockpit hatch

was transformed into a serious addition to the Allied ranks. At the time of the collapse in 1940, Valin was in Brazil as part of the French military mission. He opted to join de Gaulle, but was not able to get to Britain until April 1941. In July he was appointed Chief of Staff of the FAFL. For his pains he was sentenced to death *in absentia* by the Vichy authorities.

Despite the relatively few personnel who opted to join the FAFL at the end of the Syrian campaign, there was now at least a base from which to begin training the new wholly French squadrons. The tiny number of aircrew in the FAFL at the end of 1941 (Valin had 186 pilots and 17 navigators) compared to the 205 Frenchmen, 546 Czechs and 1813 Poles serving in the RAF, seemed insignificant. Despite this, after some internal squabbling among the French, Valin was given authority to form autonomous units within the RAF from the end of 1941. As a reminder of what their struggle was about, these were to be named after French provinces occupied by the Germans. The fighter squadrons were the first to be formed, and were, with one notable exception, based in England.

GC IV/2 *'Ile de France'*, otherwise known as No 340 Sqn RAF, formed at Turnhouse on 7 November 1941, and incorporated within its ranks the few French naval airmen in England. It became operational by the end of that month and began sweeps over northern France from April 1942. During the air operations over Dieppe in August 1942, one of the earliest members of the unit scored his first kills. Under the *nom de guerre* Pierre Kennard, 23-year-old *Cdt* Pierre Laureys shot down two Do 217s on the 19th. He damaged an Fw 190 in November and another on 9 March 1943. He destroyed two others the same day and became an ace when he scored his last kill five days later over Le Touquet. Close to *Général de* Gaulle, Laureys had escaped on a boat full of Polish escapees on 24 June 1940, leaving his stricken parents on the quayside. In May 1941 he spoke for many when he wrote in answer to questions about why he had left, 'Why did I leave? Why did I leave all that I loved, all that made me happy? Because I still had the feeling that it was not finished, that the General who had called to us needed our combat abilities in the future and that I preferred to die rather than live under German occupation'. Postwar he founded and edited *Aviation Magazine* until 1968.

Several members of *'Ile de France'* later gained fame with the *Normandie Niémen*, including Marcel Albert and Didier Beguin (who returned to command the unit in March 1944 after destroying eight aircraft in Russia, only to be killed by flak on 26 November). On D-Day, 6 June 1944, *'Ile de France'* gave fighter cover to the invasion forces, and from February 1945 they were a part of 2nd TAF until they returned to the control of the *Armée de l'Air* on 25 November 1945.

The origins of the second French RAF squadron, GC III/2 *'Alsace'*, or No 341 Sqn RAF, lay in Free French Flight No 2 in the Middle East. Originally formed in September 1941 under the command of Jean Tulasne, it served with distinction in the North African campaign until March 1942, when it was decided that the unit would be sent back to England. General Rommel intervened, however, and it was not until September 1942 that the personnel were ready for their return. In the meantime, de Gaulle had persuaded the Soviet authorities to accept a French-manned unit on the Eastern Front. As a result, the men were re-directed to that unit, while *'Alsace'* was then reformed in England, commanded by René Mouchotte, as No 341 Sqn in January 1943.

Equipped with Spitfires, the squadron began sweeps over France from Biggin Hill in March 1943. It remained in southern England on similar duties until D-Day, where it gave fighter cover. In August 1944 it moved to France, and then to Belgium the following month. Most of the late-war missions were directed against enemy ground forces. On 8 November 1945 the men returned to the *Armée de l'Air*.

One of the first members of the new unit in England was Michel

Bernard Duperier views his recently-applied personal emblem on the engine cowling of his Spitfire Mk VB BM324 of GC IV/2 *'Ile de France'* (No 340 Sqn) on 19 August 1942. The ace used this aircraft to claim one and one shared kills, one probable and one damaged – the damaged and shared claims (both Do 217s) were scored over the Dieppe beachhead on the day this photo was taken

Boudier who, already having three confirmed kills to his name scored while he was with *'Ile de France'*, was given command of the *2e escadrille* of *'Alsace'* – even though part of the RAF, the French retained the same system of organisation in the two *Groupes*. By D-Day he had added four more confirmed kills and two probables to his score, but on 9 July 1944, just after he had shot down a Bf 109 for his eighth and last confirmed victory, he was downed himself by a USAAF Thunderbolt. After evading capture for three weeks, Boudier was captured by the Gestapo and sentenced to death. He so impressed his captors by his defiance, however, that he was instead imprisoned in Germany until the end of the war. In 1946 he went to Indo-China on active service for two years, before returning to take up ever more senior positions, ending as a colonel with 4th ATAF in 1962. Boudier died after a long illness in 1963. He was 43.

A compatriot of Michel Boudier was Marcel Bouguen, one of the few French aces who did not qualify as a pilot in his homeland. In September 1941 Bouguen obtained his RAF pilot's wings and was soon posted to *'Ile de France'*. On 1 December 1942 he obtained his first confirmed victory over an enemy aircraft, an Fw 190 off Cherbourg. At the end of January 1943 he was posted to the newly-formed *'Alsace'* where, between May and September, he added four more victories. Promoted to *Capitaine* on 1 Jan 1944, Bouguen was killed on 9 March when the bomb his Spitfire was carrying blew up on its rack during a practice attack.

One of the more perceptive members of *'Alsace'* was Jacques Andrieux, who although a pilot from 1937, saw no action in France in 1940. After a daring escape from Brittany in December that year, he was sent to Odiham. Posted to No 130 Sqn in September 1941, he took part in shipping attacks, often on heavily armed flak ships. He later wrote two books about his experiences, sating in one of them, 'the most difficult thing in war is to begin again the next day'. During the summer of 1942 Andrieux had several inconclusive combats, and his first confirmed success was not until 28 February 1943 when he destroyed an Fw 190 off Cherbourg. In June 1944 he joined *'Alsace'*, and by the end of the war he had six confirmed and four probable kills. While Andrieux had survived the war, he discovered on his return to his family that the Nazis had executed his father. Postwar, he was one of the first jet pilots, and retired as a general in 1970.

Despite the relatively small number of French personnel in the RAF compared to say the Poles, they were nothing if not versatile. Bernarnd Duperier, born in 1907, had already served for three years as a pilot during his national service before being recalled again in 1939. Escaping to England (via the USA) in 1941, he joined the FAFL. After scoring with the RAF, he became CO of GC 2 *'Ile de France'* in April 1942. By January 1943 Duperier had seven confirmed kills and a probable. After returning from a mission to Canada in December 1943, he took command of No 341 Sqn *'Alsace'* in August 1944. Although remaining with the squadron, Duperier led the Biggin Hill Fighter Wing for a time, the only Frenchman ever to command a frontline RAF Wing. On 4 August 1944 *Cdt* Duperier parachuted into France to liaise with the Resistance. He was wounded two days later and spent a year in hospital. Postwar, he was very active in civil aviation and became President of the *Aéro-Club de France*.

Two other fighter squadrons were formed under the RAF, No 329 Sqn, or GC I/2 *'Cicognes'*, and No 345 Sqn, or alternatively GC II/2 *'Berry'*. Both were on Spitfires in early 1944 from personnel who had previously served with the Vichy forces in North Africa.

The redoubtable Jean Accart commanded GC II/2 (No 345 Sqn) until his posting to the USA in December 1944, although he did not score any more victories. Back in 1937, Léon Vuillemain had served under Accart in GC I/5. Now he rejoined his old friend and squadron commander in *'Berry'*. On 11 May 1940, the *patrouille* consisting of the pair, and François Morel, had jointly shot down an He 111. All three became aces while serving during the Battle of France, although Morel was shot down and killed on 18 May after ten confirmed and two probables. When Vuillemain joined No 345 Sqn he had eleven confirmed and four probables, one of his victims being a Wellington downed off Port Lyautey on 28 August 1942. He was to score no victories with the RAF, as the unit was mainly committed to ground attack sorties. Vuillemain retired as a lieutenant colonel in March 1962 and died on 10 October 1974.

Although not technically a fighter ace, the famous pre-war aviator and author Antoine de Saint Exupéry flew a number of hazardous photo-recce missions in the F-5A Lightnings of Esc 2/33 over the south of France in late 1944. He is seen here taxiing out for another mission. As a reserve officer in the *Armée de l'Air*, Saint Exupéry had flown reconnaissance missions in Potez 63s and Bloch 174s during both the 'Phoney War' and the Battle of France, before demobilisation following the Armistice. After spending two years in the USA, Saint Exupéry returned to his old reconnaissance unit in North Africa in June 1943 and flew two missions before being declared unfit for operational flying (he was 43 years old, and in poor physical shape). However, he was returned to flying status by no less an individual than Gen Ira Eaker, Commander of the US Air Forces in the Mediterranean. Cleared to fly a further five missions, Saint Exupéry successfully completed eight from Bastia before being shot down into the sea by two pre-production Fw 190D-9s on 31 July 1944 off St Raphael. His body was never found

This 13-page colour section profiles many of the aircraft flown by the leading French aces of World War 2, as well as the mounts of some of the lesser known pilots who scored five or more kills. All the artwork has been specially commissioned for this volume, and profile/unit insignia artist Mark Rolfe and figure artist Mike Chappell have gone to great pains to illustrate the aircraft, and their pilots, as accurately as possible following exhaustive research by the author. The majority of the 39 aircraft depicted in profile over the following pages have never been illustrated in colour before. Indeed, this volume features the largest number of colour profiles pertaining to the aircraft flown by French aces published to date.

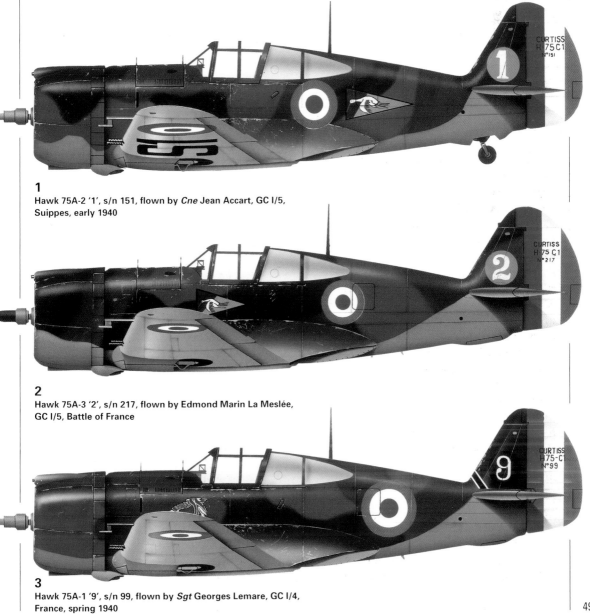

1
Hawk 75A-2 '1', s/n 151, flown by *Cne* Jean Accart, GC I/5, Suippes, early 1940

2
Hawk 75A-3 '2', s/n 217, flown by Edmond Marin La Meslée, GC I/5, Battle of France

3
Hawk 75A-1 '9', s/n 99, flown by *Sgt* Georges Lemare, GC I/4, France, spring 1940

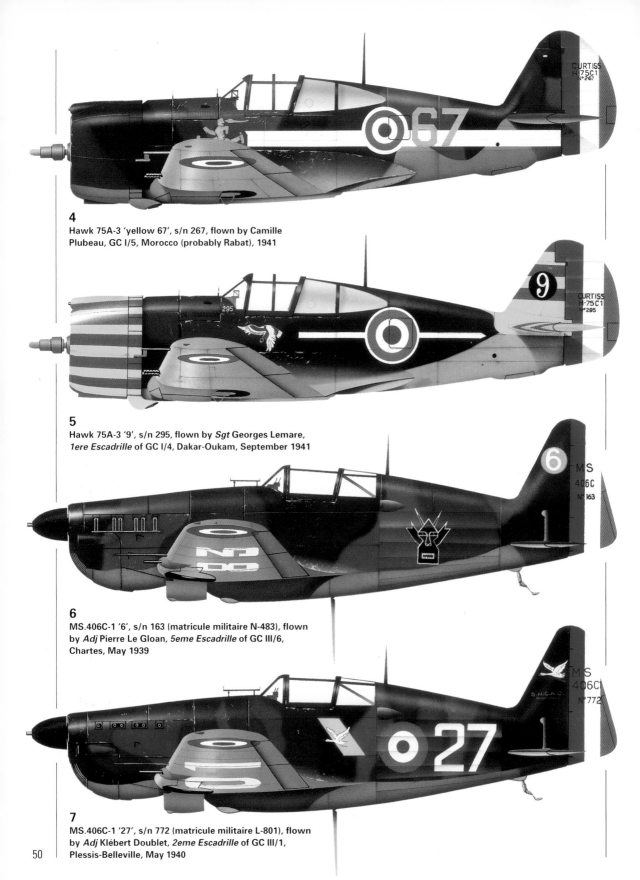

4
Hawk 75A-3 'yellow 67', s/n 267, flown by Camille
Plubeau, GC I/5, Morocco (probably Rabat), 1941

5
Hawk 75A-3 '9', s/n 295, flown by *Sgt* Georges Lemare,
1ere Escadrille of GC I/4, Dakar-Oukam, September 1941

6
MS.406C-1 '6', s/n 163 (matricule militaire N-483), flown
by *Adj* Pierre Le Gloan, *5eme Escadrille* of GC III/6,
Chartes, May 1939

7
MS.406C-1 '27', s/n 772 (matricule militaire L-801), flown
by *Adj* Klébert Doublet, *2eme Escadrille* of GC III/1,
Plessis-Belleville, May 1940

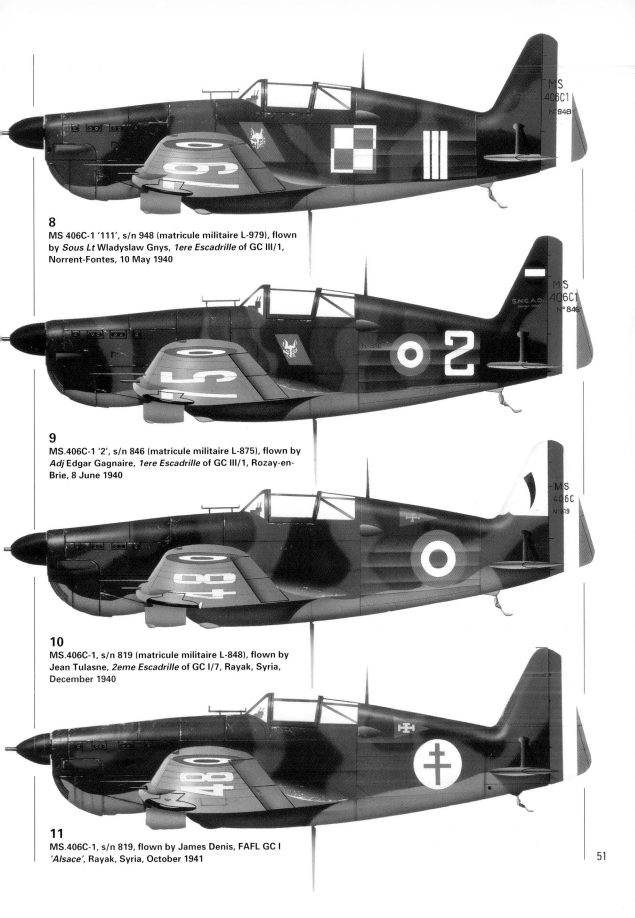

8
MS 406C-1 '111', s/n 948 (matricule militaire L-979), flown
by *Sous Lt* Wladyslaw Gnys, *1ere Escadrille* of GC III/1,
Norrent-Fontes, 10 May 1940

9
MS.406C-1 '2', s/n 846 (matricule militaire L-875), flown by
Adj Edgar Gagnaire, *1ere Escadrille* of GC III/1, Rozay-en-
Brie, 8 June 1940

10
MS.406C-1, s/n 819 (matricule militaire L-848), flown by
Jean Tulasne, *2eme Escadrille* of GC I/7, Rayak, Syria,
December 1940

11
MS.406C-1, s/n 819, flown by James Denis, FAFL GC I
'Alsace', Rayak, Syria, October 1941

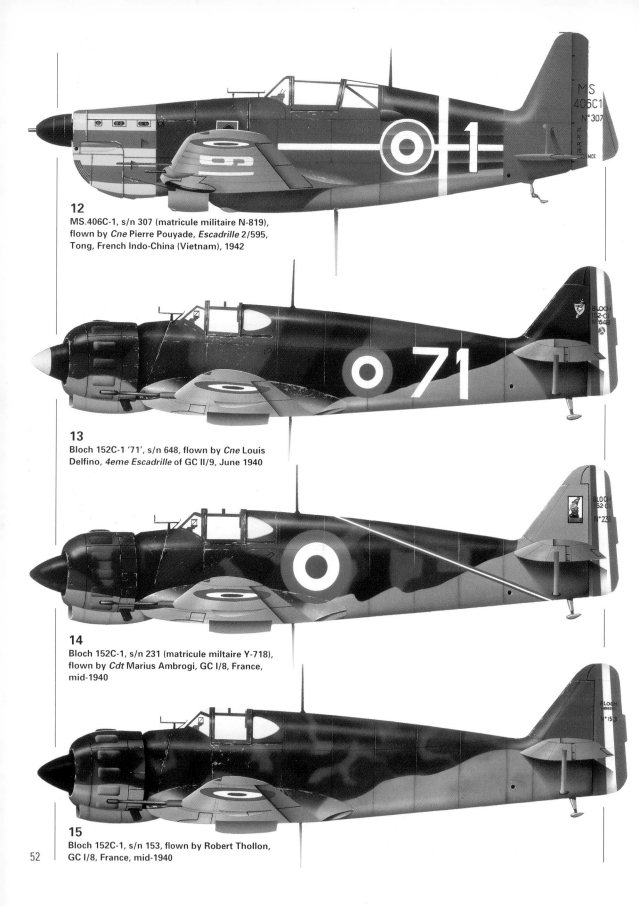

12
MS.406C-1, s/n 307 (matricule militaire N-819),
flown by *Cne* Pierre Pouyade, *Escadrille* 2/595,
Tong, French Indo-China (Vietnam), 1942

13
Bloch 152C-1 '71', s/n 648, flown by *Cne* Louis
Delfino, *4eme Escadrille* of GC II/9, June 1940

14
Bloch 152C-1, s/n 231 (matricule miltaire Y-718),
flown by *Cdt* Marius Ambrogi, GC I/8, France,
mid-1940

15
Bloch 152C-1, s/n 153, flown by Robert Thollon,
GC I/8, France, mid-1940

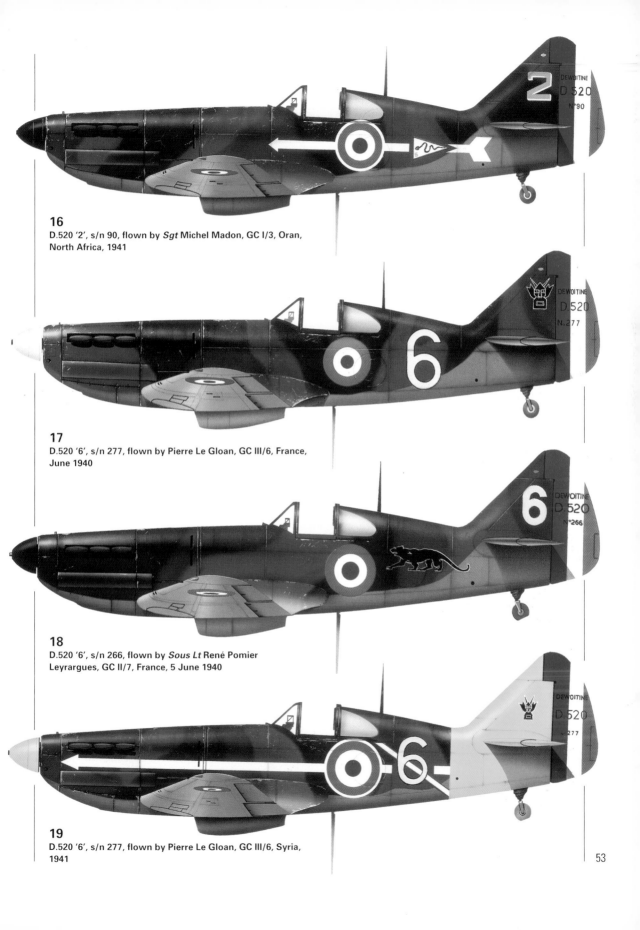

16
D.520 '2', s/n 90, flown by *Sgt* Michel Madon, GC I/3, Oran,
North Africa, 1941

17
D.520 '6', s/n 277, flown by Pierre Le Gloan, GC III/6, France,
June 1940

18
D.520 '6', s/n 266, flown by *Sous Lt* René Pomier
Leyrargues, GC II/7, France, 5 June 1940

19
D.520 '6', s/n 277, flown by Pierre Le Gloan, GC III/6, Syria,
1941

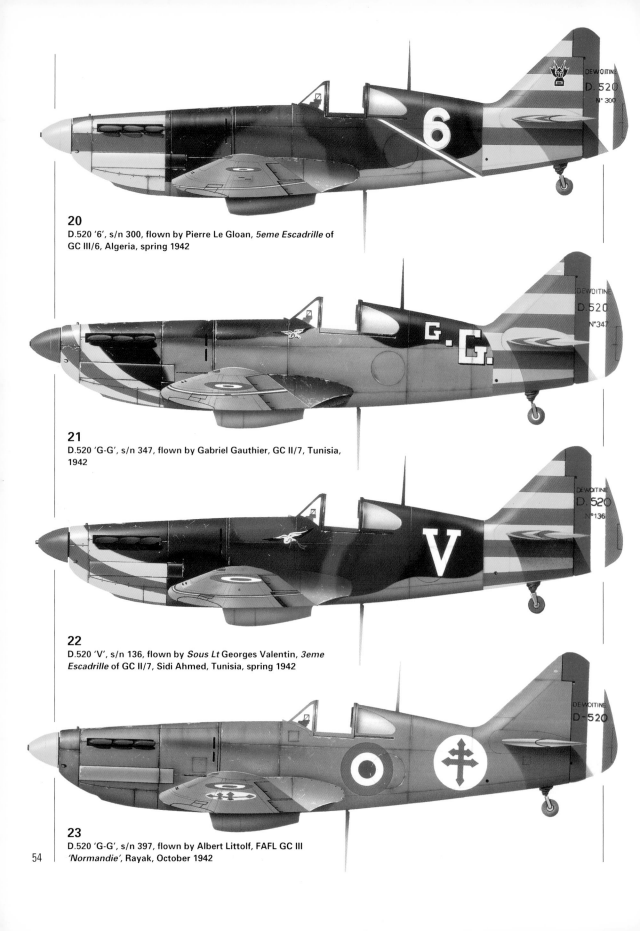

20
D.520 '6', s/n 300, flown by Pierre Le Gloan, *5eme Escadrille* of
GC III/6, Algeria, spring 1942

21
D.520 'G-G', s/n 347, flown by Gabriel Gauthier, GC II/7, Tunisia,
1942

22
D.520 'V', s/n 136, flown by *Sous Lt* Georges Valentin, *3eme
Escadrille* of GC II/7, Sidi Ahmed, Tunisia, spring 1942

23
D.520 'G-G', s/n 397, flown by Albert Littolf, FAFL GC III
'Normandie', Rayak, October 1942

24
D.520 'G-G', s/n 347, flown by Gabriel Gauthier, GC II/7,
Tunisia, summer 1941

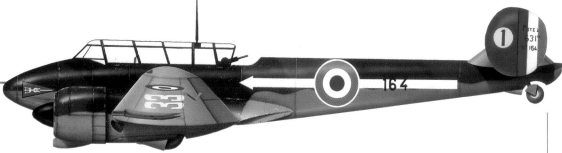

25
Potez 631 No 164 (matricule militaire X-933), flown by Pierre Pouyade, ECN IV/13, France, summer 1940

26
Spitfire Mk VB BM324, flown by *Cdt* Bernard Duperier, GC IV/2 *'Ile de France'*/No 340 Sqn, Hornchurch, 19 August 1942

27
F-5A Lightning (serial unknown), flown by Antoine de Saint Exupery, 1st *Escadrille* of GR II/33, Bastia, Corsica, Spring 1944

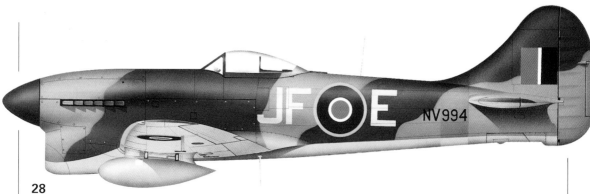

28
Tempest Mk V NV994, flown by flown by Flt Lt P H Clostermann, No 3 Sqn, Hopsten (B.112), April 1945

29
Hurricane Mk I (Trop) Z4797, flown by Jean Tulasne and probably Albert Littolf, FAFL GC I 'Alsace', Fuka, Western Desert, May 1942

30
Hurricane Mk II (Trop) 'S' (serial unknown), flown by Lt Camille Plubeau, possibly from the fighter school at Meknes, Morocco, 1944

31
Yak-1 '44', flown by Marcel Albert, GC III 'Normandie', Ivanovo, Russia, April 1943

32
Yak-1 '11', flown by Albert Durand, GC III *'Normandie'*, Orel, Russia, May 1943

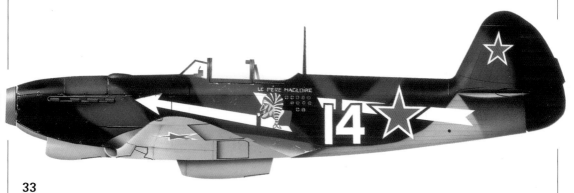

33
Yak-9 '14', flown by Marcel Lefèvre, GC III *'Normandie'*, Sloboda, Russia, October 1943

34
Yak-9 '60', flown by René Challe, GC III *'Normandie'*, Dubrovka, Russia, June 1944

35
Yak-9 '5', flown by Roger Sauvage, GC III *'Normandie'*, Toula, Russia, May 1944

36
Yak-9 'Yellow 35', flown by Jacques André, GC III *'Normandie'*, Toula, Russia, winter 1943-44

37
Yak-3 '1', flown by René Challe, *1ere Escadrille 'Rouen'* of GC III *'Normandie-Niémen'*,
East Prussia, December 1944-17 January 1945

38
Yak-3 '6', flown by Marcel Albert, GC III *'Normandie-Niémen'*, East Prussia, late 1944

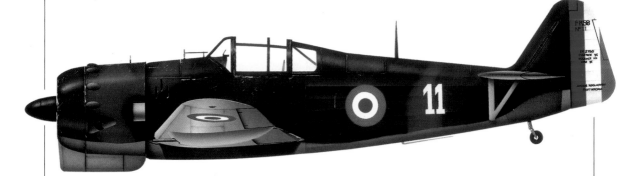

39
FK.58 '11', S/N 11, in service with *Ecole de Chasse* at either Lyon-Bron or Montpellier just after the June 1940 Armistice

1
Sous Lt Edmond Marin La Meslée
of GC I/5, seen in late 1939 in
France

2
Sous Lt Pierre Le Gloan of GC III/6,
Athens-Eleusis in May 1941, en route
to Syria

3
Commandant Pierre Pouyade, third
CO of GC III (the *Normandie-Niémen*
Regiment) in Russia in 1943-44

4
Czech ace *Capitaine* Alois Vasatko,
who served with GC I/5 in France in
May 1940

5
Sous Lt Georges Pissotte of GC III/2
in northern France in the winter of
1939-40

6
Commandant Bernard Duperier of
GC IV/2 *'Île de France'*/No 340 Sqn
at Hornchurch in mid-1942

1
Egyptian vulture
emblem of SPA 153.

2
SPA 67

3
SPA 155 (the 'Petit Poucet')

4
SPA 78

5
SPA 73 (the 'Cicognes')

6
GC III/6,
5th *Escadrille*

7
SPA 88

8
SPA 82

9
SPA 84

10
SPA 93

11
Escadrille 2/595

12
C46

13
'Cross of Lorraine' of
the *Forces Françaises
Libres*

14
Personal emblem of
Cdt Bernard Duperier

15
Unidentified, but
presumably that of
the fighter school at
Meknes, Morocco

16
GC II/9,
4e Escadrille

17
Personal emblem of
Marcel Lefèvre

18
GC III/7,
6e Escadrille

IN SOVIET SKIES

It was in Russia that the most famous of all the Free French squadrons served. Officially, the unit – to be known as GC III of the FAFL – had its foundation in Damascus, Syria, on 1 September 1942. This was where volunteers from the exiles in England and the Middle East gathered under the command of *Cdt* Pouliquen (second in command was *Cdt* Jean Tulasne, of whom more later). It was quickly decided in accordance with FAFL policy that the unit would be named *'Normandie'*. During the Battle of Stalingrad, while the Soviet administration slowly sorted out the many details for their passage to Russia, the pilots began training in October of 1942 at Rayak with two worn out D.520s. Finally, on 11 November the *'Normandie'* volunteers embarked on three Dakotas and began their tortuous journey to Russia. On 29 November, in the middle of the Russian winter, the men eventually arrived at their training base at Ivanovo. There, true to their word, the Russians offered the French pilots their choice of equipment – Russian, British or American.

The choice of aircraft was made by Jean Tulasne. After trying various types, he chose the Yak-1 on account of its manoeuvrability, reminiscent of the D.520, much to the pleasure of the Russians. Conversion training began immediately on the two-seat Yak-7. On 22 February 1943 Jean Tulasne became CO when *Cdt* Pouliquen was posted to the French military mission in Moscow. The unit went operational soon after.

Jean Tulasne does not figure in the list of French fighter aces, yet this account would be incomplete without recording the influence of his personality upon the *'Normandie'* Group.

Born on 27 October 1912, Tulasne's father and two uncles were all airmen. Despite the death of his father in a landing accident in 1929, Tulasne decided to become a pilot too. Gaining his brevet in 1933, he showed exceptional talent as a pilot, consequently serving as an instructor for a year. He was unable to take part in the defence of France as he had been posted to command the *2e escadrille* of GC I/7 in Syria. Refusing to accept the orders of Vichy, Tulasne arranged his own 'disappearance' over the sea on 5 December 1940 and flew to join the

Cdt **Pierre Pouyade poses in front of his Yak 9 with his two Russian mechanics. Pouyade was the third CO of the *Normandie Regiment* in Russia**

FFL in Palestine. After combat service with the RAF, he was instrumental in gathering together many of the men who formed the basis for the *'Normandie'*. Tulasne's evident piloting and diplomatic skills ultimately led to him being placed in command of the unit.

On 22 March 1943 13 Yak 1s of the new *'Normandie'* took off for their operational base at Polotniani-Zavod, south-west of Moscow, just as the Red Army launched a major offensive. On 5 April, while escorting Pe-2 bombers, Préziosi and Durand each shot down an Fw 190 as the first victories by French pilots in Russia. *Sous Lt* Albert Durand had also scored the first kill (an He 111) for his old unit, GC III/1, on 10 May 1940, with three more confirmed and a probable coming before he decamped from Oran on 14 October 1941, accompanied by Marcel Lefèvre and Marcel Albert, to join the FFL. After numerous missions with *'Ile de France'* in England, he decided to try his luck in Russia. Durand scored six more confirmed kills there before his death in action on 1 September 1943.

Congratulated by their Russian allies, morale in the *'Normandie'* was high, but on 13 April nine aircraft, led by Tulasne, were attacked by eight Fw 190s. In a swirling dogfight three of the Germans were destroyed, but three of the Yaks were downed in flames, all the pilots (Derville, Poznanski and Bizien) being lost. Realising the need to restore morale by getting his men back into action as quickly as possible, Tulasne arranged joint missions with Soviet Guards units, fighter sweeps and bomber escort missions throughout April. He flew three or more missions a day himself and by 20 May, when the unit moved to Kozielsk, *'Normandie'* had eight victories confirmed, but had lost another pilot as a PoW.

The unit next moved to Khationki, where it flew alongside the 18th Guards Fighter Regiment. The French pilots were billeted in a village some four kilometres from the airfield except for Jean Tulasne, who preferred a dugout near his aircraft in order to be able to take-off as quickly as possible in case of an alert. When the other pilots arrived for the dawn patrol they would find Tulasne ready and waiting, impatient to be off.

A relative calm had descended on the front by 9 June when nine reinforcement pilots arrived, led by *Cdt* Pierre Pouyade. Two weeks later the unit's score was increased when an Fw 190 was shot down by Tulasne for his first confirmed victory. The unit received a boost on 5 July when the first Yak-9s were delivered, and there was just time to familiarise themselves with the new aircraft before the battle of Kursk began on the 10th.

The first sortie for the *Groupe* was flown on 12 July when 14 Yak-9s escorted two formations of Pe 2s on an uneventful raid on the German lines. The following day they escorted 10 Il-2s sent to attack a bridge at Tsin. The target was being covered by 24 Bf 110s, which were rapidly forced to form a protective circle. In the resulting melee *Cne* Albert Littolf, Albert Durand and *Sous Lt* Noël Castelain each destroyed a German aircraft apiece. There were no losses on the Russian side.

Castelain had still been in training at the time of the French armistice, but had escaped to England. There, he had gained his wings and embarked on a series of adventures with James Denis in the Middle East. He had been one of the original volunteers for service in Russia, and in the action detailed above, he had claimed his third victory. Often flying alongside his great friend Albert Littolf, with whom he had trained in England, he had scored four more confirmed kills by 16 July when both

A rare in-flight shot of Marcel Albert flying his winter-camouflaged Yak-1M '44' from Ivanovo in early 1943. The machine wore this camouflage until April of that year

men failed to return from a mission.

July was a month of intense activity, with the *Groupe* flying several missions a day. In the same engagement in which Littolf and Castelain had been lost, Pouyade shot down a Ju 87 and Tulasne a Fw 190 for his third kill. In just four days, the *Normandie* pilots had destroyed 17 enemy aircraft in 112 sorties, but the cost had been heavy. Six pilots had been killed, among them Jean Tulasne on his 40th operational sortie. Pierre Pouyade was the last to see Tulasne, 'a few seconds later he alerted us by radio of the presence of several Fw 190s above us, in an almost pure summer sky. As he climbed into the sun the little white clouds came between us and hid him forever'.

As for Pierre Pouyade, he had six kills to his credit at the time of Tulasne's death, after which he assumed command of the *Normandie*. The Soviet authorities were greatly alarmed to discover that the unit now had only nine fit pilots, and forbade them to carry out any more combat missions without authorisation.

On 4 August the French mechanics with the unit were replaced by Russians, this decision having been made necessary due to the sheer fatigue of the former, who had been worn down by the rigours of the work, the conditions and the language. Nevertheless, replacement pilots continued to reach the unit. Most of August was taken up by training and a move to a new base at Smolensk, and by the end of the month the unit's score had crept up to 42 confirmed kills in five months of operations.

4 September saw three Ju 88s added to the bag, among the scorers being Marcel Lefèvre, the great friend of Marcel Albert and Albert Durand. The three had escaped together from Oran on 14 December 1941, and had all volunteered for Russia simultaneously. Lefèvre had not scored his first victory (an Hs 126 over Sofonovo) until 2 May 1943, but quickly proved himself to be one of the best pilots in the unit – by November he had 11 or 12 confirmed kills. When the *Groupe* moved back to its original base at Ivanovo for the winter, he was then (with Marcel Albert) tasked with training the incoming pilots, a he proved to be an exceptional instructor. In May 1944 Lefèvre and his men returned to the front, but before he could see further action he crashed at Toula on the 28th after his fighter burst into flames during a test flight. Pulled from the cockpit with severe burns, he never recovered and died on 5 June. He was 26 years old.

In October 1943 Pierre Pouyade had been posted to North Africa in search of fresh volunteers. That he was successful can be seen in some of the names which were added to the ranks in January 1944; Carbon, Mertzisen, Sauvage, Martin and Marchi, al of whom became aces. On 16 January *Col* Pouyade also returned, followed in February by eight more pilots, among them Robert Iribarne.

Born on 27 September 1918, Robert Iribarne was based in Oran with GC I/9 when war broke out, and thus never saw combat. He had then volunteered for the *'Normandie'*, and within a few days of his entry into combat in June 1944, he shot down an Fw 190. Flying throughout the summer and into the winter, Iribarne had scored seven confirmed kills (all fighters) by 18 January. He disappeared on a mission on 11 February 1945 somewhere west of Zinten, in East Prussia.

By 7 February 1944 the influx of new pilots allowed the *Groupe* to be divided into *escadrilles*. These were given names as follows: 1e *'Rouen'*; 2e *'Le Havre'* and 3e *'Cherbourg'*. A fourth *escadrille* was added in April and named *'Caen'*.

The unit had seen a significant departure on 16 February when *Cne* Didier Beguin returned to England to join GC III/2 *'Alsace'*. In eight months of combat he had scored eight confirmed kills, but was not to add to his tally before he was shot down in flames by flak on 26 November and killed. Despite this, invigorated by yet more pilots, including the brothers Challe and Georges Lemare, *'Normandie'* re-equipped with improved Yak-9s in May 1944.

On 23 June the Red Army resumed its offensive towards Vitebsk, on the Polish border. After a period of little activity the unit reopened its scoring again when Pouyade and René Challe each destroyed a Bf 109 on the 26th. That same evening, a major operation involving two formations of Yaks, one of 21 led by Pouyade, followed by 17 led by Delfino was flown. They confronted a dozen Fw 190s and shot down eight for the loss of two Yaks.

During a transfer flight to Mikountani, in Lithuania, a pilot by the name of de Seynes was carrying his chief mechanic stuffed behind him as a passenger in the fuselage. A fuel leak filled the cockpit with noxious fumes, but de Seynes refused to bale out and abandon his passenger, who had no parachute. In the ensuing crash-landing both were killed. The gallantry of the pilot made a profound impression upon the Russians.

Fighting intensified from 28 July, and the *'Normandie'* was entrusted with protecting the troops crossing the River Niémen. Exposed to flak and fighters alike, the pilots shot down two Fw 190s and a Ju 87, Jacques André chasing the latter aircraft through the flak. He claimed the dive-bomber as a probable, and returned to base but his Yak-9 never flew again. A pilot since his 15th birthday, André spent much of his early career as an instructor. He first saw action while with GC II/3 when he shot down an RAF Catalina off Oran on 18 May 1942. His next kill came was with the *Normandie* on 30 July, and by the end of the war he had scored 16 confirmed and 4 probables, and been awarded the gold star of a Hero of the Soviet Union. He died on 2 April 1988.

At the end of July *Col* Pouyade reported to his men that their unit had claimed 86 confirmed victories to the end of June, and that Stalin himself had awarded their unit the name *'Normandie-Niémen'* in recognition of their defence over the river there. On 1 August the Yak-9s received red white and blue tricolours on their spinners, and by the end of the month the first of the superb Yak 3 fighters had been delivered. By mid-September the unit had advanced to Antonovo, but the weather restricted flying, and air combats were few. Léon Cuffaut added two Bf 109s to his score on

Léon Ougloff on patrol, as seen by René Sauvage some 4000 metres above Königsberg, in East Prussia, in March 1945. Ougloff was of Russian ancestry, and scored seven victories between January and March 1945. He was subsequently killed in a Mosquito in July 1947. Ougloff is seen here flying René Challe's Yak-3 after he had been wounded and hospitalised on 17 January 1945

30 September, but as one was only a probable, he had to wait until 16 October (when he downed an Fw 190) to become an ace. By the end of that month he had 13 confirmed victories and 4 probables. Postwar, he spent much of his career in the *Armée de l'Air* on overseas assignments. He retired as a *Général de Brigade* on 20 January 1962.

A lack of enemy aircraft started to create a desire for a return to France by the *'Normandie-Niémen'* pilots, but the start of a new offensive on 13 October kept them at their posts. Suddenly, three days into the campaign the missing Luftwaffe aircraft reappeared in large numbers, and in an intense period of vicious combat over East Prussia, *'Normandie-Niémen'* had their single most successful day. In an incredible 24 hours, the unit flew 100 sorties, escorted 126 Soviet Boston and Pe 2 bombers and shot down 29 enemy aircraft confirmed, with 2 probables and 2 damaged. Not a single aircraft from the *'Normandie-Niémen'*, or their charges, was lost.

Throughout October the unit was involved in hectic fighting. An unusual victory was scored by Joseph Risso for his tenth confirmed victory on 18 October when he downed a Henschel Hs 129. Risso had decided to join the Allied cause immediately after the armistice in June 1940. Stationed in North Africa, Risso and two comrades 'borrowed' an aircraft, intending to fly to Gibraltar. Unfortunately, he force-landed in Spanish territory and was immediately jailed. With the aid of the secretary of the French military attaché, Risso was given false papers and escaped. Once in England he trained, unusually, as a nightfighter pilot, and in 1941 he joined No 253 Sqn, but desiring more action, he was one of the first to volunteer for the *'Normandie-Niémen'*. Scoring his first victory on 16 July 1943, Risso ended the war with 11 confirmed and 4 probables. Postwar he remained in the air force, retiring as a general in 1971.

The unit made multiple kills almost every day in October, and their achievements were recognised by Stalin in an order of the day on the 24th. Five days later, *'Normandie-Niémen'* suffered it final fatality of

Roger Marchi poses in front of his Yak-3 at Bourget shortly after his return to France on 20 June 1945. His 13 kills are marked just behind the cockpit. Note the oddly proportioned star

1944, although not in action, but in an accident. Jean-Jacques Manceau had been a member of the *'Normandie-Niémen'* since summer 1944, and between 26 June and 24 October he had scored six confirmed kills (all fighters). On the 29th of the month, while searching for trophies in the old German lines, he trod on a mine which blew off a foot. In falling, he set off another which virtually severed his left arm. Rushed to hospital, he could not be saved and died, a victim of gangrene, on 2 November. He was 26. On 12 December the longest serving members of the *'Normandie-Niémen'* received permission to return to France, and Cdt Louis Delfino replaced Pierre Pouyade as CO of the unit.

At the beginning of 1945 bad weather restricted most flying – at the time the unit's score stood at 202 confirmed kills. From 14 January the weather improved, and over the next few days some 36 German aircraft were shot down for the loss of a pilot. By now the *'Normandie-Niémen'* was operating from well within East Prussia, near Königsberg. Early February saw more claims, but Robert Iribarne did not return on the 11th.

On 20 February the unit moved to Wittemberg. At the same time it was gradually being reduced in size as the war neared its end, the *Groupe* shrinking to just 24 pilots in two *escadrilles*. March proved to be relatively quiet, and *Général* Petit, visiting the regiment, announced the formation of a second *Groupe* at Toula – 17 pilots were already under training there.

On 27 March the *'Normandie-Niémen'* participated in one of its last major combats of the war when three Fw 190s and two Bf 109s were downed near Pillau for the loss of *Sous Lt* Maurice Challe. The elder of the two brothers who served in the unit, Maurice was 33 at the time of his death. He had escaped to Spain, but had been held in prison there for six months before being returned to Casablanca in December 1943, where he joined his brother René in their journey to Russia. He had ten confirmed kills and one probable to his name at the time of his death. In this same combat fellow ace François de Geoffre de Chabrignac was also shot down. Wishing to join the FFL in June 1940, he had attempted to escape from his unit in Oran by stealing an aircraft, but was caught and jailed. Released after *Torch*, he flew P-40s for a time before joining the *'Normandie-Niémen'* in January 1944. Once in the USSR, de Chabrignac claimed seven kills in five months, the last falling the day before he was himself shot down into the freezing Baltic. Remarkably, he was rescued by Russian soldiers, and became something of an adventurer postwar.

On 7 April the unit moved to Bladiau, where they were shelled on the ground by German artillery six days later, causing the *Groupe's* last fatality of the war when Aspirant Henry was killed by shrapnel. Ironically, he had scored the last aerial victory for the *'Normandie-Niémen'* (an Fw 190) only the day before. On the 24th yet more replacement pilots arrived, and the veterans were notified of their return to France on the 30th.

On 8 May 1945 World War 2 finally ended, but the unit was not stood down until the following day. There was now the matter of a serious campaign of awards ceremonies, feasts, toasts and parades to endure, before the unit learned that they could take their aircraft home in return for their assistance in the war. This they did, but not until 20 June 1945 when 37 Yak-3s landed at Bourget. In 4534 flying hours and 869 combats they had scored 273 aerial victories and 37 probables, but had lost 42 pilots killed or missing. For the *'Normandie-Niémen'* the war was truly over.

ACES AND VICTORIES

To France goes the honour of producing the world's first fighter aces – Eugene Gilbert and Adolphe Pegoud – in World War 1. With a fine regard for recognising this new form of warfare, and the consequent awards to the pilots, the number of aerial victories required by a pilot to achieve 'ace' status was quickly formalised by the French and set at five. This has become the generally accepted norm in France, Britain and America, but varied in other countries, particularly in the Luftwaffe in World War 2, where the minimum number of victories required by a pilot to be recognised as an *'Experte'* could be as high as ten or more.

For a pilot aspiring to become an 'ace', he had to be able to produce proof of his claims. For a French pilot in 1914-1918 it was necessary for wreckage or independent ground witnesses to confirm his claims. Unlike the RFC, no victory was awarded on the say-so of the pilot alone, nor for that rather nebulous category 'driven down out of control'. Consequently, the French claims for World War 1 relate only to confirmed kills. In World War 2, however, for some reason it was decided to allow pilots to claim 'probable' kills, but these did not count toward the total needed for the status of 'ace'. Shared victories were treated as a whole and added to the pilot's score, but only the one victory was added to the unit tally.

On this basis, it has to be said, many of the French pilots have higher scores than if they had been tabulated under RAF, USAAF or Luftwaffe rules. Thus it is more difficult to compare the true number of victories attributed to individuals within the *Armée de l'Air*. Recent research reveals how notoriously difficult it is to confirm the numbers of aerial victories claimed by any nation in World War 2. In France, until 10 May 1940, it was relatively straightforward to confirm pilots' claims as enemy aircraft mostly fell on French soil but the chaos accompanying events on the ground in that summer, when many of the French fighter aces made their reputations, rendered it much more difficult. The victory scores given here, therefore, are those officially recorded by the SHAA. Even so, controversy still smoulders with regard to the true achievements of the French pilots during the Battle of France. Suffice it to say that the French airmen generally fought well for their country, despite the handicap of poor tactics, an incompetent High Command and indifferent equipment. The Battle of France was lost, but it was lost on the ground.

The careers of most of the French fighter aces of 1939-45 differ from those of almost all the other combatant nations by virtue of the complex political issues which attended the French collapse in 1940. When *Marshal* Pétain created the government of Vichy, overnight he divided the nation and set Frenchman against Frenchman. How much the talk of 'treachery' within France, which had led to the defeat or 'betrayal' by the British at Dunkirk and Mers el Kebir, influenced the decision by many to support Pétain is debatable. History favours the defiance of the enigmatic

Général Charles de Gaulle and those who shared his opposition to the collaborationists, yet, strictly speaking, the legitimate government of France was that headed by Pétain. During the war this situation caused much bitterness, with those who joined de Gaulle either being hailed as patriots or reviled as traitors, while those who chose to stay and fight on the German side were labelled as heroes or turncoats – twice over if they later joined the Allies. Outside France this unhappy situation has left some ambivalence towards those who served Vichy, even though they may have later joined the ranks of the Free French. It is probably fairest to say that each believed he was serving his country in the way he thought best.

In a book of this size it is not possible to give pen portraits of more than a few aces. Those that follow are an arbitrary selection chosen to give an idea of the conditions and events which were familiar to many of them. It is worth noting that most of them were NCOs at the outbreak of war.

Jean Accart

One of the most popular of the French fighter aces, Jean Accart was born on 7 April 1912 in Fécamp. After qualifying as a marine navigator in 1931, he served aboard the French transatlantic passenger liners *France* and *Ile de France*. Called up for military service in 1932, he was serving on the cruiser *Bretagne* when he volunteered for service with the *Aéronautique Maritime* – the French equivalent of the Fleet Air Arm. He subsequently qualified as a land-based pilot at Avord on 8 March 1933 and as a flying-boat pilot on 3 June at Hourtin. After a spell flying the CAMS 37, Accart opted to transfer to the *Armée de l'Air*, whereupon he joined the 5th *Escadre de Chasse* at Lyon-Bron in January 1936. By the outbreak of war, *Lt* Accart was flying Hawks with *escadrille* SPA 67 of GC I/5.

This unit claimed 71 aerial victories during the Battle of France, now *Capitaine* Jean Accart being credited with a dozen of these confirmed and four probables. Possibly of even more significance, and a measure of this modest man, the unit had lost only one pilot in action. His career as a fighter pilot was ended on 1 June 1940 when, accompanied by his wingman, the Czech *Adj* Frantisek Perina, Accart was instructed to intercept a group of Luftwaffe bombers returning from a mission near Châteauroux. Finding himself unable to make contact with his ground station (French radios and fighter direction techniques not being the best), he joined up with a patrol of D.520s to intercept another Luftwaffe raid on Bâle. While attacking a He 111 he was struck by return fire when a bullet penetrated between his eyes and lodged in his skull – the absence of armoured windscreens on French fighters cost the *Armée de l'Air* dearly. With barely enough strength to leave the cockpit of his Hawk, he parachuted and reached the ground unconscious, injuring his left arm and leg in the process. The Franco-German

Capitaine Jean Accart, commander of GC I/5, shows how close he came to injury on 13 May 1940 when a Heinkel rear gunner fought back. He was not so lucky on 1 June. In both cases he would have avoided injury if only his Hawk had been fitted with an armoured windscreen

armistice came into effect while he was recovering from his injuries, after which he was tasked with the creation of the fighter training school at Selon de Provence. Later, when the whole of France was occupied by the Germans, Accart escaped to Spain. There, he was initially imprisoned, but was released and travelled to North Africa, where the Free French authorities made use of his experience by asking him to form a fighter group. This he did, receiving command of GC 2/2 *'Berry'* (aka No 345 Sqn). Equipped with Spitfires, the squadron later served with distinction over Normandy, Arnhem and Germany. In December 1944 Jean Accart was sent to the USA for staff training at Fort Leavenworth, returning in 1945 as a *commandant* to join the inspection-general staff of the *Armée de l'Air*. Postwar, Jean Accart enjoyed a distinguished career with NATO and SHAPE, retiring as a general on 1 July 1973. He died on 19 August 1992.

Marcel Albert

Officially the second-ranking ace, Marcel Albert was born on 25 November 1917 in Paris into a family of modest means. Obliged to work for Renault to support his studies in the evening, and his dream of flying, he joined the *Armée de l'Air* on 7 December 1938 and was still undergoing advanced training when the war broke out. Posted to GC I/3, he downed his first confirmed aircraft (a Do 17) on 14 May 1940. Albert was given a 'probable' against an He 111 six days later, but did not score again until 1943 – he personally believed that his first kill was a Bf 109 which was not confirmed. Following the signature of the armistice in North Africa, he escaped with Albert Durand and Marcel Lefèvre to Gibraltar on 14 October 1941. They journeyed on to England, and GC IV/2 *'Ile de France'* (No 340 Sqn), with whom Albert flew 47 missions over northern France.

In August 1942 *Aspirant* Marcel Albert volunteered for service with the *Groupe 'Normandie'* in Russia, flying Yak fighters. He described the communist aircraft in the following terms;

A group of pilots pose in front of an early production D.520. Holding onto the propeller is *Sgt* Marcel Albert, who scored one victory with the fighter on 14 May 1940 while with GC I/3. He claimed the rest of his 23 kills on various Yak types while with the *Normandie-Niémen* in Russia

'Lighter and faster than the Spitfire V, I have managed to push it to 340 miles (per hour); more manoeuvrable than the Fw 190, which could perhaps climb better than us. With an engine comparable to an Hispano-Suiza, which never worked badly, and an axial cannon. I flew the Yak-1, then the Yak-9 and Yak-3; I never knew how the Russians numbered them. In any case, between the -1 and -9 there was a difference of some 40-50 kmh. The -9 in plan looked a little like a Messerschmitt. The Yak-3 had a range some 80-100 km more than the -9, between 590-690 km. The armament never changed – two machine guns and a cannon.'

On 16 June 1943 Albert downed his first aircraft in Russia (an Fw 189) over Brusna-Mekovaia, and in July he claimed three more, all fighters, to make 'ace'. September saw him take part in the massive air battles so typical of the Eastern Front at that time, and by year end his score had reached 15 confirmed and 2 probables. There was no uncertainty over the remaining eight kills he added by the end of the war, for all were confirmed. Immediately postwar Albert served briefly in Prague as the air attaché, before leaving the *Armée de l'Air* and emigrating to the USA.

Pierre Boillot

Pierre Boillot was born on 22 June 1918 at Laissey. A career airman, he gained his 'brevet' (wings) on 7 July 1938 and was posted to the 4th *escadrille* of GC II/7 in May 1939, and was at Luxeuil when hostilities opened in September. Like the rest of his unit, *Sergent* Boillot was responsible for the protection of the reconnaissance aircraft of the various units based within their operational area – the banks of the River Rhine extending from Rhinau to Bâle. Flying the MS.406, his first brush with the enemy (a Do 17) in November 1939 was inconclusive, and it was not until early in the morning of 20 April 1940 that he opened his score, downing a Bf 109E of 2./JG 54 over Belfort. On 10 May he shared in the destruction of his first He 111, following this the next day with a Ju 88 as a probable. During June he was credited with a share in another He 111 and a Do 17, which raised him to the status of ace. GC II/7 then retreated to North Africa, where it re-equipped with the D.520.

The unit remained there until November 1942, charged with protecting Tunisia. Operation *Torch* allowed the unit to join the Allied side, and it took part mostly in routine convoy escort and coastal patrol duties, although Boillot managed to add two Italian Macchi C.202s and a Bf 109 to his score. It was not until September 1943 that *Sergent-Chef* Boillot and his unit were chosen to land on Corsica, from where he operated in support of the Allied landings in the south of France (Operation *Dragoon*). During October he claimed two Ju 88s shot down into the sea off Ajaccio. Throughout autumn of 1944 and spring of 1945, Boillot, now a *Sous-Lt*, harried the retreating Germans over the valleys of the Rhône, adding four more Bf 109s to his score, to make his final total 13 confirmed and one probable. Postwar, Boillot remained in the *Armée de l'Air*, seeing further active service in Algeria, before retiring in 1974 as a colonel.

René Challe

The younger of two brothers who both served with distinction in the *Armée de l'Air*, René Challe was born on 6 June 1913 in Besançon. A graduate of the Saint-Cyr military academy in 1935, he first joined a

Moroccan 'tirailleur' regiment, but transferred to the *Armée de l'Air* on 1 October 1937. *Sous Lt* Challe received his wings on his 25th birthday, and several months later was posted to GC III/7, then flying the MS.406.

At the outbreak of war, the now *Lt* Challe was adjutant to the commander of the 5e *escadrille*, which hampered his combat opportunities until 9 May 1940, when he claimed a He 111 as a probable east of Vitry. On the 15th, during a savage battle against a formation of Do 17s, he had just downed one when he was severely injured by a bullet in his right lung. He managed to extricate himself from his blazing fighter and landed close to a French artillery unit. Challe was evacuated to hospital at Bar-le-Duc, from where he witnessed the collapse of the French army.

Demobilised in November 1942, he determined to leave France and take up the fight against the Germans wherever he could. Accompanied by his brother Maurice, on 11 August 1943 the two made their escape to Spain, where they were at first imprisoned. In December they were handed over to the Free French authorities in Casablanca, where they expressed their wish to join the *'Normandie'* regiment in Russia. Asked in later years why they chose that unit, René Challe recounted in *Icare*;

'There were a number of fighter pilots from the 1939-40 campaign. Many felt they had a score to settle with the Luftwaffe once they had learnt better techniques; others fought against the fate which had kept them from combat for various reasons. For us, the offer of the Soviet High Command to give the French pilots their best equipment, to serve as a French unit and at the same time to get the chance for effective combat against the Germans was a magnificent opportunity to take our revenge.'

So it was in this spirit that they arrived at Toula on 18 March 1944. Warmly greeted by their new comrades, they began training on the Yak-9. Challe seized his first chance for combat over Soviet soil on 26 June when he destroyed a Bf 109 some 50 km west of Vitebsk. It was in October, however, that *Capitaine* Challe was given his opportunity for revenge. In 12 days, between 10-22 of that month, he shot down three Fw 190s and two Bf 109s to become an ace. On 16 December he exchanged command of the 4th *escadrille* for that of the 1st, and it was in this capacity that he flew his last mission on the Eastern Front on 17 January 1945, when destroyed an Fw 190 north-east of Gumbinnen. This ninth, and last, victory was to cost him as dearly as his first as, outnumbered, he was shot down by another Fw 190 and seriously wounded in his left arm. Nevertheless, he managed to make it back to his own lines and land at his own base. There, he fought vigorously to prevent his arm being amputated, an action which appeared inevitable

The Challe brothers, René (left) and Maurice, in front of the former's Yak-9 in June 1944. 'No 60' carries the 'fury's head' emblem of René's old unit, GC III/7, with which he had served in France in 1939-40. René Challe disappeared on a mission over East Prussia on 27 March 1945

to his surgeon. In the event his arguments prevailed. At the Liberation, *Cdt* Challe was posted to the provisional government of the new French Republic. Postwar, he occupied a number of important command and teaching posts, before joining the staff of the Inspector-General of the *Armée de l'Air*, from where he retired as a full colonel in 1964.

Louis Delfino

Another of the great aces who served with the *'Normandie-Niémen'*, and one of very few pilots to enjoy success on the unfortunate Bloch 152, Louis Delfino was born on 15 October 1912 in Nice. Tragedy came early to Delfino when his father was killed in World War 1. Like René Challe, Delfino was a graduate of Saint-Cyr. Promoted *Sous Lt* on 1 September 1933, he joined the *Armée de l'Air* and received his wings on 27 July 1934. Posted to the reconnaissance arm, Delfino secured a posting to fighters as France prepared for war in 1938, joining GC I/4 at Reims. From 27 August 1939 (now a *Capitaine* and adjutant of the *Groupe)*, he spent the 'Phoney War' based at Wez-Thuisy, where he saw little action.

On 10 May his unit moved to Dunkirk-Mardyck, and the next day a He 111 was comprehensively shot down by eight pilots of GC I/4, among them Louis Delfino. That same day he was awarded a 'probable' Bf 109, and the same again on the 13th. On the 17th, he was transferred to Buc to command the 4e *escadrille* of GC II/9, equipped with Bloch 152s, in defence of Paris. During one of his few free moments, he designed the famous 'Morietur' emblem of his new unit. It was not until the 26th that Delfino was able to add to his score when he shot down a Bf 109 and an Hs 126. Then, in five days between 5 and 10 June, he brought down an He 111 and three Hs 126s, plus a Do 17 as a 'probable', taking his total to seven confirmed and three probables. Despite the heroic efforts of the French fighter pilots, events on the ground led to the armistice of 22 June.

For the next two years Delfino remained loyal to his unit until on 29 May 1942 he was posted back to his original *Groupe*, GC I/4, stationed at Dakar. His only claim for the period came on 12 August 1942 when Delfino, and the 2e *escadrille,* downed an RAF Wellington off Dakar. Following *Torch,* a visit to the unit on 5 January 1943 by Free French *General* Giraud saw GC I/4 join the Allied camp. Hoping to receive P-39 Airacobras, Delfino was disappointed to learn that his unit was to re-equip with Martin Marylands for coastal patrol duties so, on 11 January 1944, he volunteered to join the *Normandie Niémen*.

Arriving in Russia on 28 February, he was promoted to *Commandant* four months later, and rapidly familiarised himself with the Yak-3 – regarded by its pilots as the best fighter in the world. On 16 October the *Normandie* began the great offensive into East Prussia. That day Delfino shot down a Bf 109 for his ninth confirmed victory, with an Fw 190 as a probable. A week later he claimed two more Fw 190s, one being confirmed and the other remaining a probable. In a period of intense combat, on the 22nd he destroyed another Fw 190, with a Bf 109 as a probable on the 26th. Promoted to second in command of the *Groupe* on 12 November, he was to score four more victories (all fighters) before the end of the war. On 26 April 1945 he was promoted to lieutenant-colonel, eventually returning to France at the head of the *Normandie Niémen* on 20 June. In the postwar years, Louis Delfino held successively more important posts in the

Armée de l'Air, culminating in his appointment as Inspector-General of the force on 1 January 1964. He died suddenly on 11 June 1968 of a heart attack having spent 37 years in the service of the *Armée de l'Air*.

Albert Durand

Born on 16 September 1918 in Grasse, Albert Durand joined the *Armée de l'Air* at Nîmes in April 1938 and showed early promise as a pilot, gaining his brevet on 29 July. He was posted to his first operational unit in August 1939 when, as a *Sergent*, he joined GC III/1 at Beauvais. Equipped with the MS.406, the unit moved soon afterwards to Chantilly, tasked with air defence of the capital. There was little action during the period of the *'drôle de guerre'*, and even a move to Lorraine for escort duties for the reconnaissance aircraft of the 3rd Army saw no change.

Consequently it was not until 10 May 1940 that Albert Durand first engaged in combat, opening the score for his unit by forcing an He 111 to crash-land on the beach north of Calais. On 18 May he shared in the destruction of a Do 17 near Rozoy-sur-Serre, following this the next day with a Bf 109 as a probable. On the 20th he destroyed a Ju 88 dive-bombing near Compiègne, and his last victory of the Battle of France was a Ju 87 downed near Aumale. Following the armistice, GC III/1 was disbanded and Durand was given leave until 11 March 1941, when he was posted to Oran with GC I/3, then flying the D.520.

Like Marcel Lefèvre and Marcel Albert, Durand found his new situation far from satisfactory, and the thought of shooting down British aircraft was insupportable. Consequently, by means of a ruse, all three decamped to Gibraltar with their aircraft on 14 October 1941 – as a curious consequence of this event their former unit was re-numbered GC III/3. Arriving in England on 19 June 1942, he retrained with the RAF before joining No 340 Sqn/*'Ile de France'* for fighter sweeps over the Channel and northern France. Soon afterwards, he embarked for Russia with Lefèvre, bound for the *Normandie* regiment. Following a conversion course on the Yak-1, *Sous Lt* Durand was graded as 'exceptional' by *Cdt* Tulasne, who was responsible for training the *Normandie* pilots.

On 5 April 1943 Durand shot down an Fw 190 near Roslav, followed by another on the 13th. On 5 May he shared an Hs 126 with *Cne* Littolf, and it was not until 13 July did he score again when he downed a Bf 110 for his eighth confirmed kill. Three days later he shared a Fw 189, downed near Krasnikovo, and on the last day of August 1943 he destroyed an He 111 and damaged an Fw 190. However, on 1 September Durand simply disappeared while on a mission. He was 25 years old.

Gabriel Gauthier

Born into a family of doctors on 12 September 1916 at Lyon, Gabriel Gauthier was naturally expected to also take up the profession. Interested in military matters from his early teens, a career in military medicine seemed to be a logical choice. Finding, however, that he was more interested in sport, he eventually opted for a career in aviation. After initially failing his exams, he joined the *Armée de l'Air* in 1936. Finally, in October 1938, he was posted to GC II/7, then flying MS.406s.

On 28 August 1939 Gauthier's unit moved to Luxeuil, ready to oppose the Luftwaffe in the war which was now inevitable. The pilots were full of

Cdt Jean Tulasne (right) briefs Albert Durand in front of the latter's Yak-1, complete with sharksmouth. The location for this photograph is Kosalsk in May 1943. As far as is known this was the only such marked aircraft in the *Normandie-Niémen* Regiment

confidence, believing that the Germans could never best them. Gauthier's first taste of success came when he shared in the destruction of a Do 17 of 4.(F)/121. A month later, on 21 December, while escorting a reconnaissance Potez 63/II, his unit engaged a dozen Bf 109s. While observing the crash of one fighter that he had just shot down, his aircraft was seriously damaged by another which had latched on to his tail. Gauthier was seriously wounded in the ensuing crash, and did not return to operations until long after the armistice.

When he eventually rejoined his unit, it had moved to North Africa, where it was re-equipped with Spitfires in late 1943. It was while flying in support of operations over Corsica that he added to his score, destroying two Ju 88s and damaging two others, shooting down a Do 217 and a Savoia Marchetti SM.79 and claiming another Ju 88 as a probable between 28 September and 17 December 1943. Promoted to *Capitaine*, and given command of the 2e *escadrille*, he took part in operations in support of the landings in Provence, where he was again shot down and wounded, this time by flak. He was saved from the Gestapo by members of the Resistance, who eventually got him safely into Switzerland. Recovered, he again rejoined his unit in time to share in the destruction of five more Bf 109s and a probable between Christmas Eve 1944 and the end of the war.

Postwar, he was sent to America for staff training, before returning to France to occupy progressively more senior positions in the *Armée de l'Air*. This culminated on 1 December 1969 when he was appointed Chief of Staff, a position he held until his retirement in December 1972.

Edmond Guillaume

One of the older fighter pilots of the wartime *Armée de l'Air*, Edmond Guillaume was born on 31 January 1904 at Ozoir-la-Ferrière. He gained his wings in autumn 1924, and for many years afterward served in the *Aéronautique Militaire* as a flight instructor, only slowly climbing the promotion ladder. A week before the outbreak of war, *Lt* Guillaume was called to active service with GC I/4, but it was not until the beginning of the Battle of France that he opened his score, sharing in the downing of an He 111 over Belgium on 11 May 1940. Although 36 years of age,

Guillaume rapidly demonstrated his fighting ability with two Bf 109s shot down on 17 May (one shared). In a masterful display of flying at the controls of his Hawk, he downed two more on the 26th, watched with admiration by his squadron mates. Now an ace, he shared an Bf 109 on 5 June, and then claimed another destroyed, and a probable, the next day. Promoted to *Capitaine* in September, he spent the rest of the war passing on his experience to several other units, eventually finishing with GC III/6 when he was demobilised in August 1945. By then he had amassed 1042 flying hours, 115 of them in combat. Not well known, Guillaume is typical of many of the gritty professionals at the core of any army.

Pierre Le Gloan

Possibly the French fighter ace best known to the British, the enigmatic Pierre le Gloan came from a humble background. Born the son of a peasant in Kergrist-Moëlou on 6 January 1913, Le Gloan obtained a state scholarship in order to satisfy his passion for aviation, and allow him to join the *Aéronautique Militaire* in December 1931. On 7 August 1932 *Caporal* Le Gloan received his brevet. Volunteering to extend his service resulted in a posting to the 6e *escadre de chasse* in September 1933. In gunnery practice he was among the best in the group, and his ability to lead a formation led to *Sgt Le* Gloan being appointed to *'chef de patrouille'* (flight leader) on 20 October 1936. In February 1938 he was recognised as a career NCO, and went with his unit to North Africa.

On 1 May 1939 GC III/6 was formed at Chartres, *Sgt Chef* Le Gloan becoming a member of the 5th *escadrille*. Equipped with the MS.406, the unit transferred to Betz-Bouillancy on 4 September 1939 with the task of protecting Paris and the lower Seine. The monotony of the *'drôle de guerre'*, and the absence of any real action, sapped the morale of the unit until 15 November, when GC III/6 moved to Wez-Thuisy in the ZOAN. Eight days later, in company with Robert Martin, Le Gloan downed a Do 17P of 5.(F)/122 near Verdun, thereby opening the score for GC III/6.

There followed a long period of waiting, broken only by intermittent false alarms, and it was not until 2 March 1940 that, again with Martin, he scored the his unit's second victory – another Do 17 south-east of Bouzonville. On 11 May he shared in the destruction of a He 111, as well as claiming a second as a probable. Three days later he was again given a share in downing yet another He 111. At the end of May GC III/6 withdrew to re-equip with the D.520.

On 10 June Mussolini decided to attack France as well, and three days later *Adj Le* Gloan downed two Italian Fiat BR.20 bombers. Two days later there followed the episode which was to give him immortality when he became only the second pilot in World War 2 to claim five victories in a single sortie – namely four Fiat CR.42 biplane fighters and another BR.20. With 11 confirmed kills, Le Gloan was now the premier ace of his *Groupe*.

'6' was regarded by Pierre Le Gloan as his lucky number, and he is seen here as a *Sgt Chef* in front of his MS.406, s/n 597 (matricule militaire L-536), in which he scored his first aerial victory (a Do 17) on 23 November 1939. The African mask emblem of the *5eme Escadrille* of GC III/6 is clearly visible

When the Franco-German armistice came into effect, Le Gloan and his unit retired to North Africa. In May 1941 GC III/6 was ordered to participate with the Germans in operations in Vichy-controlled Syria, where the bitter fratricidal struggle between Vichy and the Free French was to erupt into a bloody confrontation. In the event, the Germans found they had more pressing concerns, and left the defence of Syria and the Lebanon entirely in the hands of the Vichy authorities. In a campaign lasting little over a month, *Sous Lt* Le Gloan downed six RAF Hurricanes and a Gladiator to take his score to 18 confirmed and three probables.

Following Operation *Torch*, the remaining Vichy forces in North Africa at last joined the Allied camp. Among them was *Lt* Pierre Le Gloan. On 13 August 1943 he was given command of the 3e *escadrille* of his Groupe, now re-named *'Roussillon'* and equipped with P-39 Airacobras. It was at this point that Le Gloan's obsession with flying was to cost him his life. On 11 September (the anniversary of the death of legendary World War 1 ace Georges Guynemer, which most other pilots were commemorating) Le Gloan and *Sgt* Colcomb took off early in the morning for a coastal escort mission. As they crossed the coastline Colcomb noticed that Le Gloan's P-39 was emitting black smoke. Returning to base, the engine suddenly stopped and the ace attempted a forced landing. Unbeknown to either pilot, Le Gloan's belly drop tank had failed to release and the instant he hit the ground his aircraft blew up in a fiery explosion.

Albert Littolf

Fired by a passion for aviation of almost religious proportions, Albert Littolf was born on 31 October 1911 in Cornimont. One of eight children, he resolved at an early age that the only way to better himself was through flying. Joining the *Aéronautique Militaire*, he obtained his wings on 31 July 1931 and passed out first in his class. Posted to the 7e *Escadre* at Dijon, his flying abilities were soon recognised by his commanding officer, who had formed an aerobatic team and included Littolf in it.

A brief posting to North Africa in 1939 with GC II/7 was not to Littolf's liking, and he requested a transfer back to France. So it was that he was with GC III/7 when the German forces broke through at Sedan, and on 12 May 1940 he shared in the destruction of a Ju 88 with his wingman. Flying one of the earliest D.520s, Littolf then shot down five Hs 126s and a probable Bf 109 (all shared) in less than a month.

Frustrated by the Armistice, Littolf and two colleagues, responding to the appeals of de Gaulle, flew from Francazal to England, where they landed almost out of fuel. There, he was one of the first six pilots to form 1e *escadrille* of the Free French GC III/2 on 13 December 1940. Soon afterwards this unit was sent to reinforce No 80 Sqn in Egypt. In the confusion of the desert theatre, Littolf also served with No 73 Sqn, seeing action over Athens, Alexandria and Tobruk – on 5 May 1941 he downed four Bf 109s over Tobruk while with the latter unit. At month end, he shared a Ju 88 kill and damaged an Italian Cant Z.1007 off Crete.

Recalled to Britain in March 1942, Littolf met *Cne* Jean Tulasne again, who was by then recruiting for the new GC 3 (the future *'Normandie Niémen'*). After training at Ivanovo throughout the winter months, the *'Normandie'* eventually reached the front on 22 March 1943. An intense man, Littolf was recalled by one his comrades;

'He lived the life of an ascetic; while we passed the long nights of the Russian winter playing poker, he stayed in his room and drew futuristic aeroplanes. He was committed to aviation as others are to religion . . . Nothing else interested him, not drinking, smoking or women. He strove to invent the ideal aircraft, and when he talked to me of his ideas, I made my objections from the point of view of the mechanics. In the end he said to me "I will never forget you after the war. . ."'

Littolf reopened his scoring by destroying an Hs 126 and a Fw 189 in May. Although the region was relatively quiet following the German defeat at Stalingrad, the French pilots found themselves occupying two exposed salients in the Orel and Kharkov sectors, near Kursk. On 5 July the Germans launched their offensive on Kursk, which developed into the largest tank battle ever seen. The Soviets, however, had full knowledge of the German plans and stopped the offensive within four days. At Khationski, where the *'Normandie'* had been immobilised since 10 July due to artillery barrages, events suddenly accelerated. As the Russians launched their counter-offensive on the 14th, the French pilots fought alongside the VVS's 18th and 303rd fighter regiments to cover their advance. Littolf destroyed a Bf 110 on the 13th and a second near Krasnikovo on the 16th, but was then posted missing after his second mission of the day.

Twelve years later the body of Albert Littolf was discovered and returned home for burial in October 1960. *'Mort pour la France'*.

Michel Madon

Another of the pilots who obeyed the orders of the post-Armistice French government to resist all aggression against French interests, Michel Madon was born on 10 January 1918 at Dijon. Entering the *Armée de l'Air* in summer 1938, he passed through various pilot schools until he was eventually posted in February 1940 to GC I/3 at Cannes, which was then waiting to convert from the MS.406 to the far superior D.520. Fortunately for Madon and his comrades, their distance from the frontline gave them time to properly train on their new mounts.

In the event *Sous Lt* Madon and his unit were posted to Suippes on 13 May to take part in the Battle of France. Within hours they were in combat over the bridges spanning the Meuse, and Madon had destroyed his first aircraft (a Bf 110). Between 6 and 16 June he made full use of his new fighter, downing four Hs 126s, a Do 17 and a Bf 109, with a second *Emil* and an He 111 as probables. This made him leading ace in his *Groupe*.

Two days later GC I/3 retreated first to Oran, then to Tunisia. There, Madon was one of many who chose to support Vichy. Promoted to command of the 1e *escadrille* on 10 November 1941, he saw no further action until November 1942, when the Allies landed in Morocco. On the 8th of that month he shared in the destruction of two or three C-47s and a Sea Hurricane. Following the conclusion of the North African campaign, Madon was posted to GC II/7 'Nice' in April 1943, where he stayed until joining GC I/7 *'Provence'*, flying Spitfires, in September. On 26 November 1943 he probably destroyed a Do 217 and damaged two Focke-Wulf Fw 200s, bringing his tally to 11 confirmed and 4 probables. After taking part in operations to liberate Corsica, Madon suffered an engine failure over Italy on 2 June 1944 and opted to bale out into a raging sea rather than fall into enemy hands. He was not found for some time.

At war's end Madon went back to France, only to be sent to Indo-China days later. There followed a series of staff and command positions until, in September 1970, he became Inspector General of the *Armée de l'Air*. A terrible accident on 14 April 1972 killed his wife, and Madon was devastated. He never recovered and died a month later on 16 May.

Edmond Marin La Meslée

The most successful of all the French pilots who participated in the Battle of France, Marin La Meslée was born in Valenciennes on 5 February 1912. After high school, he studied at the Morane flying school and gained his pilot's brevet on 1 August 1931. Pre-empting his call-up, he volunteered for a reserve officers' course in November that year, passing out as a *Sous Lt* on 20 September 1932. La Meslée was then posted to the 2nd *Regiment de Chasse* in Strasbourg, and at the end of his year's service, he signed on for a further two years – with the rank of *Sergent*. In September 1936 he decided to make a career with the *Armée de l'Air*, being posted as a *Sous Lt* in October 1937 to SPA 67, then part of GC I/5. He was flying Hawks with *Cne* Jean Accart in this unit when war broke out.

By 27 July 1939 GC I/5 had moved to its operational base at Suippes. For the next six months Marin La Meslée waited for an opportunity to carry out the job he was trained for. Contacts with the enemy were rare at that time, and it was not until 11 January 1940 that he finally caught a Do 17P of 3.(F)/11 over Verdun, bringing it down, with the help of *Sous Lt* Rey, near the German border. He described the action as follows;

'I was on patrol with my wingman, *Sous Lt* Rey, at 8000 metres when I suddenly spotted a splendid Do 17, heading for Belgium about 200 metres below us and two kilometres away. I warned my wingman, then placed the sun at my back and attacked from astern. The German machine-gunner opened fire when I was about 400 metres away. I manoeuvred to throw him off his aim, closing all the time, and opened fire at 200 metres. I gave him several bursts, closing right in until I had to break off and let my wingman have his turn. The German gunner was firing at me all the time, but his bullets went wide. I could see my own bullets hitting the fuselage and engines, and debris struck my aircraft.

'The Dornier flew straight on, and I came in for a second attack. More debris hit my aircraft, and oil spattered my windscreen. I thought that I had been hit and broke away, but just as Rey was preparing to fire the Dornier went into a vertical dive. He must have been hit pretty badly, because he was losing fuel and his engines were belching smoke. Rey fired in the dive, broke away, and I took over. The Dornier levelled out at 2000 metres, then went into a dive once more and turned towards the frontier. We took it in turns to fire at him, not giving him a moment's respite. The German gunner was still firing, and it seemed likely that the Dornier might escape, because we were very

The foremost French fighter ace of 1940, Edmond Marin La Meslée is seen in the cockpit of his six-gun Hawk 75A-3 s/n 217, with the emblem of the *1ere Escadrille* of GC I/5 beneath the cockpit

close to the border. I remember shouting words of encouragement to my wingman. We were now very close to the ground, so close in fact that I had to break off an attack. A moment later, I had the immense satisfaction of seeing the Dornier make a belly landing in a field. On returning to base I learned that he had come down only a kilometre from the frontier; the crew had been taken prisoner, and only one of them was wounded. My aircraft was unscathed, although my wingman's had been hit five times.'

His next victories were gained on 12 May, two days before the German assault began in earnest, when his *patrouille* caught some 20 Ju 87s dive-bombing French infantry in the Ardennes. Catching the Stukas without fighter cover, slaughter ensued. A dozen were claimed by GC I/5, three being confirmed, and a fourth downgraded to a probable, for La Meslée himself. The next day he got a Bf 109. From 15 to 26 May he saw constant action as attempts were made to halt the invasion. On the 15th he shared an Hs 126, the next day a Do 215, on the 18th three He 111s out of a formation of 21 and on the 19th another Heinkel bomber. There was a brief 'lull' until the 24th, when he downed an Hs 126 near Saint-Loup, with another shared the next day. This was followed by an He 111 on the 26th, which La Meslée shared with eight other pilots from his *escadrille*. Always outnumbered, he frequently returned with his Hawk full of holes, and in recognition of his fighting spirit, La Meslée assumed command of his *Groupe* after Jean Accart was hospitalised on 1 June.

The battle was being lost, but the fight was not yet over. On 3 June he shared in the destruction of an Hs 126, with a Do 17 as a probable, and four days later, over Soissons, he claimed two more probables (a Ju 88 and another Hs 126). There was no uncertainty over his last kill, however, the Ju 88 crashing near Chatillon sur Bar on the 10th to give him 16 confirmed and four probables. By 25 June GC I/5 was in Algeria.

For the next two-and-a-half years, Marin La Meslée waited for his opportunity to resume the fight. After the 'Torch' landings, his *Groupe* re-equipped with P-39 Airacobras and carried out convoy escort and coastal patrols. In winter 1944-45 his unit was at last able to take part in liberating his homeland, and on 4 February 1945 *Cdt* Marin La Mesée led his unit, now named *'Champagne'* and flying P-47 Thunderbolts, in an attack on a German vehicle convoy in the Hart forest. On his first pass, a vehicle burst into flames, giving off dense smoke which obscured his vision. As he attempted to climb away he was hit by a 40 mm shell and crashed. Pulled from his cockpit by the Germans, he was found to have received a fatal shrapnel wound to the head. Today, a gigantic stone star in the style of the French pilot's badge marks the place where he fell.

Eugeniusz Nowakiewicz

Among the ranks of the *Armée de l'Air's* Battle of France aces are several who are not French at all. After the fall of Poland, many Polish airmen fled to France in order to continue the fight, among them Eugeniusz Nowakiewicz. Born on 2 January 1919 at Jaslo, little is known of his previous service in the Polish air force, except that he held the rank of senior private. After arriving in France, he volunteered for service with the *Armée de l'Air* and was posted to GC II/7, which he joined on 29 March 1940. Flying an MS.406, *Caporal Chef* Novakiewicz, noted for his tenacity in combat, opened his score with a shared He 111 on 11 May.

He followed this with a Do 215 'probable' over Germany on the 25th. On 1 June he knocked down another He 111, with two more Do 215s confirmed on the 5th and 10th. His final victory was a Do 17, again over Germany. With the French collapse he escaped again, this time to England, where he joined the RAF. All that is known of his later career is that he served with No 302 Sqn from 1 August 1940 until 2 July 1942 (with the rank of flying officer from 19 June that year), when he disappeared.

Frantisek Perina

Other refugees from Nazi oppression to find temporary sanctuary in France were the Czechs, among them Frantisek Perina. Born in Mokruvky on 8 April 1911, he joined the Czech Air Force in 1929. He represented his country, flying an Avia B.534, in the Zurich International Military Competition, where he was regarded as being one of the best marksmen. Following the German occupation of Czechoslovakia, he escaped in 1939, making his way to the French Foreign Legion before joining the *Armée de l'Air* as a Sergent. Promoted to *Lt,* he joined Accart's GC I/5, flying several times as Accart's wingman.

On 10 May the pair downed four Do 17s between them, following this the next day with an He 111. The 12th was the great day when GC I/5 knocked down a dozen Ju 87s, Perina's personal score being two confirmed and two probables. On the 18th he shared another He 111, and another the day after with the redoubtable Marin La Meslée. A week later another He 111 suffered at the hands of GC I/5. Perina's last victory in the Battle of France was yet another He 111, again with Jean Accart, to bring his total to 11 confirmed and 2 probables. During this action he was shot down by Bf 110s and crashed. Emerging from hospital, Perina flew his Curtiss H-75 to North Africa, but then decided to continue his personal battle and made his way to England, where he joined the RAF. With No 312 Sqn, he scored only one more victory before the end of the war.

Escaping from Czechoslovakia in 1948 after the Communist takeover, he rejoined the RAF. After his enforced retirement from flying in 1953, Perina emigrated to Canada and the USA, where he became a successful businessman. The great changes in Europe since the end of the Cold War finally enabled him to ultimately retire to his native country.

Albert Petitjean-Roget

The oldest of all the French fighter aces was born on 15 January 1903 in Toulouse. An entrant into the military academy of Saint Cyr in October 1924, he was promoted to *Sous Lt* two years later and obtained his pilot's brevet in 1927. In April 1930 *Lt* Petitjean-Roget embarked for Morocco with the 37e Aviation Regiment to take part in the operations against the rebel tribes in the Atlas Mountains. An observation specialist, he was noted for his calmness under fire, his courage and his ability to command. He left Morocco in July 1935 as a *Capitaine*, returning to France for a staff course, after which he served at GHQ, before being nominated to be military attaché in Brussels. In May 1938, *Général* Vuillemin, Chief of Staff of the *Armée de l'Air*, chose Petitjean-Roget as his ADC. Promoted to *Commandant*, his next posting was to the CIC at Chartres until, on 25 March 1940, he was given command of GC II/5, equipped with H-75s.

When the Battle of France opened in May, he quickly demonstrated his ability by downing an He 111 near Verdun. On the 20th he shared in the destruction of a Do 17, and the next day claimed an Hs 126. His last kills were on 5 (Hs 126) and 10 (Do 17) June. Evacuated to North Africa after the armistice, on 1 August he was recalled by *Général* Vuillemin to be his ADC once more. Two months later he joined *Général* Weygand's staff, where he served until he was killed in an air crash on 10 April 1941.

Camille Plubeau

One of the few fighter aces who originally wished to be a reconnaissance pilot, Camille Plubeau was born in Auxelles-Haut on 6 January 1910. A keen cyclist, he became inspired by the exploits of the likes of Lindbergh and Mermoz. Subsequently, when the time came for his military service, he applied to join the *Aéronautique Militaire*. Out of 3000 candidates, only 148 were chosen, and Plubeau was one of them. On 14 March 1929 he began his training, qualifying as a pilot on a Morane 130 on 10 August. At Istres, during his advanced training, he expressed a desire to become a reconnaissance pilot, as he 'wished to see the country'. The CO of his unit, having seen him fly, persuaded him to become a fighter pilot, however. From December 1929 until June 1932 he served in the 34th Aviation Regiment with World War 1 ace, Armand Pinsard (27 victories).

His love of travel led him to volunteer for service in Morocco in June 1932. He returned to France in December 1934, and four months later he was with GC I/5 at Lyon. In May 1939 *Adj* Plubeau was posted to GC II/4, then forming on the Hawk at Reims. By August the 'Petit Poucets' were installed at Xaffévillers in the Vosges. On 24 September he began the combat career which was to make him the *Groupe's* premier ace when he downed a Bf 109 of I./ZG 52, with another as a probable. Six days later;

'We are south-west of Bitche when my wingman waggles his wings to signify "enemy in sight". I see them immediately. He heads due south at high speed towards a Bf 109. 150 metres behind is another, and 400 metres further on, slightly higher, are three more. We have time to gain altitude and place ourselves in the sun. The enemy do not seem to have seen us. De la Chapelle attacks the leader, I take the one behind. De la Chapelle fires, the 109 turns to the right to place himself under the rest of his flight. I have to avoid the aircraft in front of me firing at my wingman. I fire a few rounds at him. He turns left. I turn also, but faster. I am quickly on his tail at a distance of 120-140 metres. I press the button, and black smoke pours from both sides of the fuselage. There is fire onboard.'

Despite this report he was only awarded a 'probable'.

There was no doubt over an Hs 126 on 31 October, and by the end of the year Plubeau had added a Do 17 confirmed and another as a 'probable'. His next victory had to wait until 11 May 1940, when he destroyed a Bf 109 – an He 111 the same day was not confirmed. On the 15th of the month he shared in the downing of a very rare Ju 86, followed by a Bf 109 by himself for good measure. Three days later he brought down three more Bf 109s and another He 111. On 6 June he destroyed another Bf 109 near Soissons, but on 9 June 1940, after bringing down another He 111 and two more Bf 109s, *Sous Lt* Plubeau was surprised by another.

His engine on fire, he waited until the last moment before parachuting to avoid being shot at in the air. Suffering from third degree burns, he was taken to hospital at Epernay, but was evacuated that same evening to

Bordeaux. Wishing to continue the fight, he landed at Algiers in August with a victory tally of 14 confirmed and four probables.

Posted to GC II/4 at Rabat, he remained there until his unit was re-equipped with Airacobras after *Torch*. Re-named *'Champagne'*, the unit was employed on convoy protection duties over the Mediterranean.

After nine months in command of the fighter school at Meknes in 1944, Plubeau was promoted to *Capitaine* and given command of the 2nd *escadrille* of GC II/9. At war's end he was in command of the training and liaison *Groupe* at Bourget, and later Villacoublay. After 155 operational missions, Camille Plubeau retired on 1 October 1946.

René Pomier Leyrargues

Despite having a combat career lasting only a few months, René Pomier Leyrargues earned the respect and admiration of his fellow pilots for two things – his unassuming character, and the fact that he shot down the German ace, Werner Mölders. Born in Montpellier on 1 November 1916, he began pilot training in 1937. In 1939 he underwent the advanced fighter course at the CIC at Chartres. On 12 March 1940 he was posted to an operational unit, GC II/7. The unit had been tasked since the outbreak of war with protecting reconnaissance aircraft operating within their sector, and due to the eerie situation of the *'drôle de guerre'*, on many occasions the two sides simply went about their business pretending not to see one another. Combats and victories were therefore rare, and during the bitter winter of 1939-40 the unit scored only six kills.

By May GC II/7 had started converting to the D.520, and on the 11th *Sous Lt* Pomier Leyrargues shared in the downing of an He 111 near Brassy. On the 19th it was a Do 17, and this was followed by two more He 111s on 24 and 25 May. By June the Panzer columns were smashing their way deep into France, and on the 5th Pomier Leyrargues was amongst eight pilots of GC II/7 that were bounced by 15 Bf 109Es of III/JG 53, led by none other than the great Werner Mölders himself, after scrambling to intercept a raid. At that time the leading German ace had 39 victories to his name, and in the ensuing dogfight, Pomier Leyrargues shot him down (Mölders apparently never saw his opponent). Another Bf 109 was claimed by the Frenchman before he was overwhelmed by weight of numbers and shot down in flames, crashing to his death in D.520 no 266 near Marissel. This fight cost GC II/7 dear, with four aircraft and two pilots lost. It was not until 1942, however, that Pomier Leyrargues' mortal remains were finally discovered and laid to rest.

Pierre Pouyade

Pierre Pouyade was that rarity among French aces by virtue of the fact that he started his combat career as a nightfighter pilot. Born in Cerisiers on 25 June 1911 into a military family, he was inevitably destined for a career in the army. A brilliant student, he came 24th out of 464 in his entrance exams for Saint Cyr, where he enrolled in 1930. Two years into his course, he decided that his future lay in aviation and gained his wings at Versailles in 1935. Lt Pouyade was then posted to the 6th *Escadre*.

In December 1936 he moved to the 4e *escadrille* of GC IV/4. Promoted to *Capitaine* in June 1939, he commanded GCN II/13 (then equipped the two-seater Potez 63) during the Battle of France. In later years he was severely critical of the aircraft and the powers that be, stating 'We had driven around throughout the winter after the German aircraft without ever being able to catch one. Why? Because the French nightfighters had made little progress since 1918. I still do not understand why the French High Command ordered and placed in service a nightfighter which was doomed to be useless'.

Despite having downed an He 111 on 20 May, the Armistice left Pouyade with a feeling of deep dissatisfaction with his attempts to defend his country. Rather than remain inactive in a France which had fallen under the control of the Germans, he volunteered for service in the colonies, with a wish to be sent there as quickly as possible. In October 1940 he received his posting to Indo-China, and on 23 November he embarked with 900 other men on a vessel intended to carry 30 civilian passengers. After 48 days at sea (26 without stopping) he reached Saigon, where, at the end of this dreadful journey, he was posted to EC II/295, flying the MS.406, where he assumed command.

Very quickly he realised that the French were collaborating with the Japanese, and obliged to scrounge to maintain both his men and aircraft, he soon received orders to attack on sight, without warning, any American aircraft flying over Tonkin. When he heard that his superiors had handed over to the Japanese an American flyer who had been shot down near the Chinese border, and who had subsequently been beheaded, he was 'totally shattered, I decided to leave, to escape'.

On 2 October 1942 he put his plan into operation. After stealing an elderly Potez 25 at Hunan, he was warmly welcomed by the Free French at Chungking. Four months later, on 5 February 1943, he landed in England. There, he received a telegram from his friend Jean Tulasne inviting him to join GC 3 (the 'Normandie Niémen' regiment), which had been in Russia for several months. After volunteering, Général Valin charged him with finding ten other pilots. This he did, and on 14 May 1943 Cdt Pouyade embarked with his men on a new voyage.

By 9 June they were in Russia, ready to take on the Luftwaffe. On Bastille Day (14 July) he shot down a Bf 110, followed the next day by a Ju 87 and a Fw 189, which brought his score to six confirmed and three probables. On 17 July he was promoted to command the 'Normandie' after the death of his friend Jean Tulasne on a mission.

In October he destroyed an Hs 126 and two Fw 190s. Apart from the dangers of combat, Pouyade also had to contend with other problems affecting his unit. Far and away the most important was the question of replacing combat casualties, and he decided to journey to North Africa in late 1943 in search of reinforcements. At the end of the war, Lt Col Pouyade, and his men, finally returned home on 20 June 1945.

Named 'Inspector of Fighters' in July 1945, and then joined the staff of President Auriol in 1947. Between 1950-53 he was military attaché in Buenos Aires, returning home as a Général. Upon his retirement in 1955 Pouyade entered politics, finally retiring from office in 1979.

Léon Richard

Léon Richard is unique among the ranks of the French aces of World War 2, as he is the only one never to have shot down a German aircraft. Born on 7 August 1910 in Paris, he gained his wings in 1929, but it was not until 1933 that he became a career NCO. On completion of his course in July 1935, he was posted to the 3e *Escadre*. In November 1937 he was given command of the reconnaissance unit GAR 571 in Algeria, and although he briefly returned to France in April 1940 to command the 1st *Escadrille* of GC I/9, he was posted to Tunisia with his unit on 6 May.

On 31 August 1940 he was in command of the 6e *Escadrille* of GC III/6 (flying D.520s), this unit playing an active part in the campaign in Syria. It was during this brief, but bitterly fought, campaign that his unique combat career began, as all seven of his victories were against the British. On 8 June 1941 he shot down a Fairey Fulmar of the Royal Navy, and the next day he destroyed a Hurricane. Friday the 13th was unlucky for a Blenheim of No 11 Sqn and its crew, which encountered Richard on that day. On the 23rd he brought down another Hurricane and a Tomahawk. Again, on 5 July, he destroyed another Hurricane, and after the withdrawal of all pro-Vichy forces from Syria, *Capitaine* Richard and his unit returned to Algeria. It was from there, while carrying out a defensive patrol, that he claimed his seventh, and last victory, a Royal Navy Fulmar, on 18 May 1942. Following the *Torch* landings, he began conversion on to the P-40(?), but on 26 May 1943 he ran out of fuel on a training flight and was killed in the subsequent violent forced landing, his skull being fractured when it struck the instrument panel.

René Roger

René Roger typifies the confusion attending the victory claims of pilots over France in 1939-40, for the official list of aces gives him five kills, whilst his unit history only four. He is included here to illustrate how the divisions in France affected individuals after the June 1940 armistice.

By the time war broke out in 1939, René Roger was one of the most experienced pilots in the *Armée de l'Air*. Born in Attiches on 4 March 1907, he was called up for his obligatory military service in 1927. Qualifying as a pilot in 1930, he became a career NCO in the *Aéronautique Militaire* in May 1931. From April 1935 until September 1939, *Adj* Roger was an instructor at Bourget. There he flew all types of aircraft, both by day and by night.

When war was declared he was posted to GC III/3, then equipped with the MS.406. For three months he occupied his time flying reconnaissance missions over Germany by day and bomber missions by night. The Battle of France gave him the opportunity to try out his fighter, and on 13 May 1940 he downed two Bf 109s in three minutes near Rosendael. Six days later he destroyed another, followed by an He 111 the following day. At this point the SHAA gives him another kill to make him an ace.

In August 1940 he was posted to GC II/3 in North Africa, and on 14 June 1941 the D.520s of the unit were transferred to Vichy-controlled Syria to resist the Allied invasion there. *Adj Chef* Roger left with them, but did not participate in the campaign, for his aircraft force-landed in Turkey on the 15th. Whether this was genuine, or a planned evasion as a result of his Gaullist sympathies, is not known. The effect was that he spent the next ten months as an assistant to the Vichy air attaché in Ankara. His attempts to obtain a commission during this time were rejected on three occasions on account of his political views, leading to him being interned for ten months between July 1942 and May 1943.

Released, he joined the Free French air force in the Middle East (and was commissioned as a *Sous Lt* in February 1944, following which he flew many missions over Syria and Lebanon between May-June 1945. Roger left the force in September with over 3000 flying hours to his credit.

Roger Sauvage

Proving that in France race was no barrier to a military career, Roger Sauvage was born on 26 March 1917, the son of a native of Martinique, killed in action in World War 1. Fascinated by aviation after reading the biography of Georges Guynemer, he joined the *Armée de l'Air* in 1935. Through most of 1937 he took part in photo-recce missions along the German border, and in April 1939 transferred to GC I/5, based at Reims.

Throughout the winter of 1939-40 he flew many escort missions, protecting observation aircraft, without ever actually being presented with the chance of air combat. When his baptism of fire finally came it almost cost him his life. While flying a twin-engined Potez 631, he caught up with a formation of three RAF Hurricanes, one of which suddenly attacked, and it was only with difficulty that he extricated himself from the cockpit of his burning aircraft. As his parachute deployed, his aircraft exploded, leaving Sauvage barely conscious as he reached the ground. For four days he lost his memory, and it was only when he regained it that he realised that the British pilot had mistaken his aircraft for a Bf 110 (this was so common an error that special markings were later applied to the Potez 631 to try to avoid such incidents). He quickly proved he had recovered by shooting down a He 111 on 18 May, although it was 16 June before Sauvage found his next victim (a Do 17) near Tours. After the armistice, he left for North Africa. While in Casablanca he was induced to leave for Russia, and the *'Normandie Niémen'*.

Arriving in the Soviet Union as part of the second contingent of volunteers in January 1944 for conversion training on the Yak-7, it was not until October that he shot down another German aircraft (an Fw 190) over East Prussia. Two days later he shared in the destruction of two Ju 87s and a Bf 109, followed by one confirmed Fw 190 and a probable 24 hours later. As the Red Army advanced through East Prussia and into Germany, *Aspirant* Sauvage added steadily to his score. Two Fw 190s on 16 January 1945, another the next day, and three more the day after that, with a fourth damaged. By 27 March 1945 – the day he destroyed one Fw 190 and damaged another near Pillau as his last victories of the war – his total stood at 16 confirmed, one probable and four damaged.

Postwar, Sauvage remained in the *Armée de l'Air*, making *Capitaine* in 1954. He wrote two autobiographies before his death in September 1977.

Josef Stehlik

Another of the expatriate Czechs who served foreign air forces so well, Josef Stehlik was born in Pikarec on 23 March 1915. He was part of the 3rd Air Regiment of the Czech Air Force when the Germans occupied his country, but escaped to France, where he was posted to GC III/3 (then flying MS.406s) just in time for the Battle of France. His first combat on 12 May was inconclusive, as he was only awarded a 'probable' Bf 110, but he shared in the destruction of two He 111s later that same day. A week later Sgt Stehlik downed an Hs 126 and a Do 17. The victory (a Do 17) which gave him ace status took place on 5 June, soon after he had converted to the D.520, followed by a Bf 110 the day after.

With the end of the fighting in France, he left for England and participated in the Battle of Britain with No 312 Sqn. Having added to his score and achieved the rank of flight lieutenant, he volunteered to join the newly formed Czech Fighter Regiment flying La-5s with the Russians. With them, he downed a Ju 87 and a Ju 88, and postwar he stayed in the new Czech Air Force as an instructor. He died on 30 May 1991.

Robert Williame

Inspired from the age of 11 by the exploits of the great French aces such as Guynemer and Fonck in World War I, Robert Williame was born on 24 February 1911 in St Martin les Boulogne. Following an uneventful but successful education, he entered Saint Cyr in 1930. In 1933 he received his pilot's wings. After advanced flying training he was eventually posted to SPA 3 (GC I/2) in 1934. Known as the 'Cicognes' (Storks) this was the successor to Guynemer's old unit. A year later Williame took the then unusual step of acquiring a parachute instructor's qualification. Recognised as being quick in word and deed, he was promoted to *Capitaine* in September 1938. By September 1939 GC I/2 was equipped with the MS.406. Based at Beauvais, Williame found the tedium of the 'phoney war' hard to deal with, and on 13 February 1940, while confined to bed with sickness, to his great chagrin, a Do 17 flew over the base.

Seeing this as a sign of action soon to come quickly raised the morale of the unit. After an uneventful mission on 22 February, and a brush with flak on 7 March, Williame and his unit engaged a Do 17 near Saverne. Although his windscreen was covered in oil, the unit was only allowed a 'probable'. The unreal atmosphere of the *'drôle de guerre'* still persisted at this time, exemplified by a curious mission on 20 April when Williame encountered some 30 Bf 109s which accompanied him to the border, neither side firing a shot. 'Incomprehensible!' he later wrote. When hostilities opened with a vengeance on 10 May, Williame and his squadron mates were still hoping that their outmoded MS.406s would soon be replaced by the D.520. On 20 May he and eight others were confronted by a large formation of Bf 109s. Williame was caught in the crossfire between two of these, and his aircraft was thoroughly shot up. Miraculously, he was untouched. On 5 June he gained his revenge when he brought down two Ju 88s, one after a chase of some 130 km. Despite the shortcomings of his mount, on 8 June, accompanied by nine D.520s and a similar number of Bloch 152s, GC I/2 intercepted a bomber formation near Beauvais, escorted by Bf 109s and Bf 110s – he downed three Bf 109s in fifteen seconds. His final score for the day was three Bf 109s and three Ju 87s to bring his ultimate victories to eight confirmed and a probable.

The announcement of the armistice devastated the pilots of GC I/2. Some spoke of burning their aircraft, others of leaving for England or crossing the Mediterranean. Williame, like many others, seems to have had little liking for the British, and crossing the Mediterranean in an MS.406 seemed too dangerous. Consequently, he stayed put. Soon afterwards his unit moved to Nîmes, where it was disbanded. On 26 October 1940, shortly after he had been given command of a new unit (GC III/9), Robert Williame disappeared on a training flight to Salon de Provence.

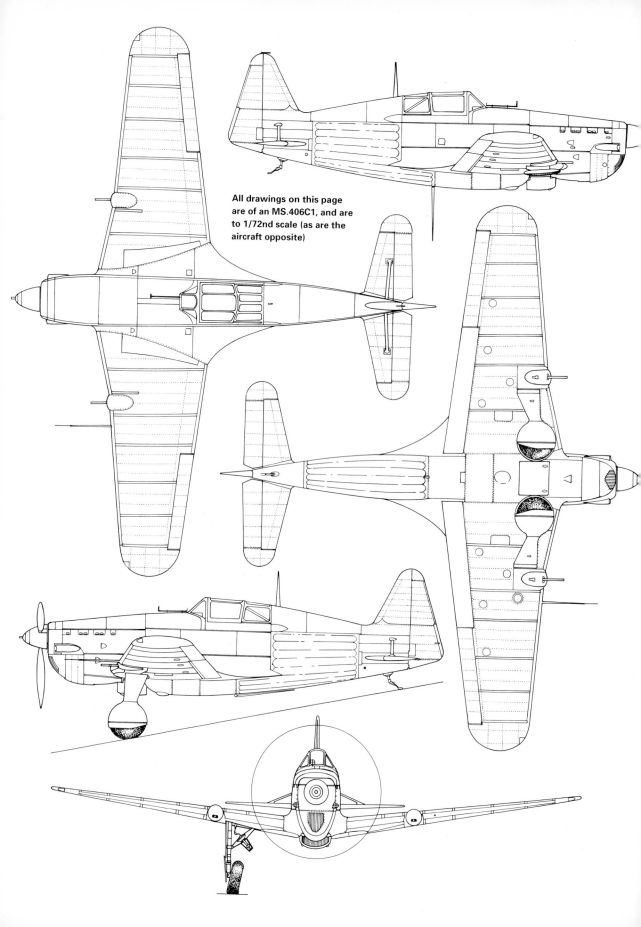

All drawings on this page
are of an MS.406C1, and are
to 1/72nd scale (as are the
aircraft opposite)

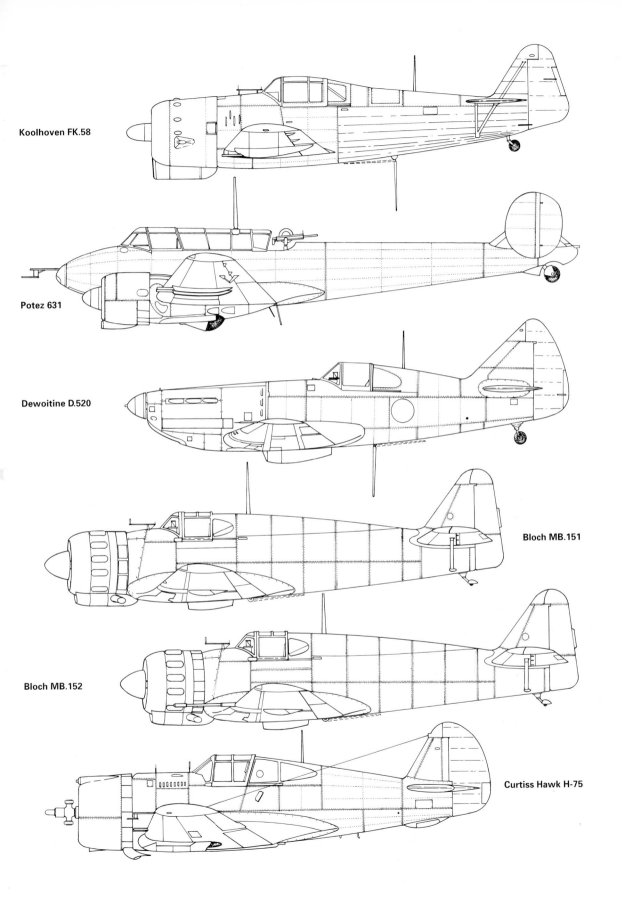

Koolhoven FK.58

Potez 631

Dewoitine D.520

Bloch MB.151

Bloch MB.152

Curtiss Hawk H-75

Appendix 1

The following is the official list of French aces, as compiled by the *Service Historique de l'Armée de l'Air*

Name	Confirmed	Probable	Name	Confirmed	Probable
Clostermann, Pierre	33	5	Tesseraud, Georges	8	4
Albert, Marcel	23	2	Doudies, Jean	8	3
Demozay (Morlaix), Jean	21	2	Carbon, Yves	8	2
Le Gloan, Pierre	18	3	Duval, Roger	8	2
André, Jacques	16	4	Warnier, François	8	2
Delfino, Louis	16	4	Amarger, Maurice	8	1
Marin La Meslée, Edmond	16	4	Challe, René	8	1
La Poype, Roland de	16	2	Foucaud, Henri	8	1
Sauvage, Roger	16	1	Mertzisen, Gabriel	8	1
Dorance, Michel	14	4	Parniere, Marcel	8	1
Littolf, Albert	14	4	Pissotte, Georges	8	1
Lorillon, Pierre	14	4	Williame, Robert	8	1
Plubeau, Camille	14	4	Moret, Antoine	8	0
Boillot, Pierre	13	1	Thollon, Robert	8	0
Lemare, Georges	13	0	Dechanet, Pierre	7	2
Marchi, Robert	13	0	Gagnaire, Edgar	7	2
Martin, Robert	13	0	de Chabrignac,		
Accart, Jean	12	4	François de Geoffre	7	2
Vasatko, Aloïs (Czech)	12	2	Monraisse, Marie Hubert	7	2
Blanck, Georges	12	1	Marie, Louis	7	2
Lefol, Georges	12	1	Paulhan, Jean	7	2
Le Nigen, Edouard	12	1	Bleton, Pierre	7	1
Madon, Michel	11	4	Charras, Marc	7	1
Risso, Joseph	11	4	Duperier, Bernard	7	1
Vuillemain, Léon	11	4	Elmlinger, Georges	7	1
Lefèvre, Marcel	11	3	Guillaume, Edmond	7	1
Perina, Frantisek (Czech)	11	2	Huvet, Robert	7	1
Valentin, Georges	11	2	La Chapelle, Antoin de	7	1
Tallent, Maurice	11	1	Leblance, Emile	7	1
Rouquette, Marcel	10	6	Rebiere, Raoul	7	1
Gauthier, Gabriel	10	2	Salès, Edouard	7	1
Morel, François	10	2	Teillet, Roger	7	1
Castin, Robert	10	1	Beguin, Didier	7	0
Challe, Maurice	10	1	Casenobe, Jean	7	0
Durand, Albert	10	1	Castelain, Nöel	7	0
Baptizet, Georges	9	4	Chesnais, Charles	7	0
Denis, James	9	4	Girou, Jean	7	0
Martin, René	9	3	Guieu, Régis	7	0
Penzini, Dominique	9	2	Hebrard, Marcel	7	0
Gouby, Robert	9	1	Iribarne, Robert	7	0
Legrand, André	9	1	Montet (Martell), Pierre	7	0
Bressieux, Jérémie	9	0	Puybusque, Jacques de	7	0
Cukr, Venceslas (Czech)	9	0	Richard, Léon	7	0
Matras, Pierre	9	0	Vybiral, Thomas (Czech)	7	0
Mourier, Yves	9	0	Andrieux, Jacques	6	4
Rey, Jean-Marie	9	0	Muselli, Gérard	6	4
Boudier, Michel	8	4	Pouyade, Pierre	6	3
Moynet, André	8	4	Coutaud, Germain	6	2

Name	Confirmed	Probable	Name	Confirmed	Probable
Hugo, Henri	6	2	Loï, Martin	5	1
Villacecque, Pierre	6	2	Nowakiewicz, Eugeniusz (Pole)	5	1
Bon, Maurice	6	1	Ougloff, Léon	5	1
Miquel, Charles	6	1	Panhard, René	5	1
Stehlik, Joseph (Czech)	6	1	Ponteins, Denis	5	1
Dorcy, Pierre	6	0	Raphenne, Henri	5	1
Doublet, Klébert	6	0	Taburet, Gaël	5	1
Hurtin, Jean	6	0	Villey, Pierre	5	1
Joire, Jules	6	0	Becquet, Emile	5	0
Manceau, Jean	6	0	Boitele, Hubert	5	0
Pomier Leyrargues, René	6	0	Dietrich, Henri	5	0
Thierry, Emile	6	0	Henry, Georges	5	0
Lamblin, Jacques	5	4	Hotellier, Jean	5	0
Romey, Maurice	5	4	Laureys (Kennard), Pierre	5	0
Grimaud, Henri	5	3	Papin Labazordierre		
Codet, Marcel	5	3	Petit Jean-Roget, Albert	5	0
Deniau, André	5	2	Planchard, Henri	5	0
Rubin, René	5	2	Roger, René	5	0
Abrioux, Paul	5	1	Satge, Marie	5	0
Bouguen, Marcel	5	1	Saussol, Roger	5	0
Garde, Georges	5	1	Starke, Robert	5	0
Krol, Waclaw (Polish)	5	1	Steunou, Marcel	5	0

Appendix 2

Aircraft and Equipment

During 1939-40 the main equipment of the French single-seat fighter *Groupes* was one of four types of aircraft – the Bloch 151/152 series, the Morane Saulnier MS.406, the Dewoitine D.520 or the American-built Curtiss Hawk 75. Other types, like the Arsenal VG.33 and Caudron C.714 (both of wooden construction), entered service, but only in very small numbers, whilst the Bloch 155 made its frontline debut in June 1940.

Of the four main types in the frontline squadrons, the MS.406 was akin to the RAF's Hurricane, with its fabric-covered tubular metal fuselage half a generation older in conception than the later monocoque D.520. The Bloch 152 never really lived up to the promise of its heavy armament, being handicapped by its mediocre engine and short range. The most effective fighter during the Battle of France was the Hawk. Although only lightly armed and relatively slow, its superb manoeuvrability enabled it to hold its own against the Bf 109E – it is worth mentioning that the Hawk was the mount of most of the aces with more than ten victories. However, the performance of these three types was such that the pilots found all too often that they could barely catch the German bombers, let alone their Messerschmitt escorts. Unquestionably the best fighter available to the French was the D.520, which combined armament, speed and dogfighting ability in a single airframe. Those pilots fortunate enough to use it in combat soon found that they could take on anything in the Luftwaffe's arsenal, with some pilots scoring dramatic victories. It was, after all, the pilot of a D.520 who downed then ranking German ace, Werner Mölders. Unfortunately for France, D.520 production lines were only just beginning to crank out aircraft as the Armistice came into effect.

Apart from the rather indifferent airframes which most French fighter pilots had to fly into combat, there were other, less obvious, factors further hindering their chances of success. One was the curious Baille Lemaire OPL RX.39 gunsight (nicknamed 'the lantern' on account of its shape), which was outclassed by both the British and German reflector gunsights. A more significant element was the absence of armoured windscreens on the French fighters. Jean Accart was just one of those who could have stayed in action longer had his aircraft been fitted with one. The third was the lack of 'punch' once the aircraft was in a favourable firing position. Both the Blochs and

Moranes had cannon, but these were relatively slow-firing, while the early Hawks boasted just four machine guns. The D.520 had only one cannon, but also four machine guns – and the performance to be able to use them to advantage.

Compared to the average RAF or Luftwaffe fighter pilot of 1940, the first thing that is apparent when looking at a French pilot is how encumbered with equipment he appeared to be. Apart from a bulky fly-ing suit, the rigid leather flying helmet, (known as a 'bombe') woollen toque and oxygen regulator all served to restrict movement within the cockpit, especially the vital glance over the shoulder.

As an aside, the throttle mechanisms on French air-craft worked in the opposite sense to those of most other nations in that pulling back on the throttle lever gave more power. This led to numerous accidents during transition training onto later Allied types.

Max Speed	Service	Ceiling	Weight (loaded)	Armament
Bloch 152	320 mph	32,800 ft	5908 lb	2 x 20 mm 2 x 7.5 mm
Curtiss 75A-3	311 mph	32,800 ft	5734 lb	6 x 7.5 mm
Dewoitine D.520	332 mph	33,620 ft	5900 lb	1 x 20 mm 4 x 7.5 mm
Morane Saulnier MS.406	304 mph	32,800 ft	5610 lb	1 x 20 mm 2 x 7.5 mm
Hurricane I	317 mph	36,000 ft	5672 lb	8 x .303 in
Spitfire I	353 mph	34,700 ft	6050 lb	8 x .303 in
Bf 109E-3	348 mph	34,450 ft	5875 lb	2 x 20 mm x 7.9 mm

Appendix 3

Organisation and Tactics

During peacetime the frontline French fighter units were organised into *Escadres*, each made up of two *Groupes*. Each *Groupe* had some 25-30 aircraft, divided into two *Escadrilles*, each with 12 aircraft – approximately the same size as an RAF squadron of the period. After the outbreak of war, the main operational unit became the *Groupe*, which offered more command flexibility.

Units were identified by abbreviations such as GC II/5. This indicated '*Groupe de Chasse* (i.e. fighter) No 2, 5th *Escadre*'. *Escadrilles* within an *Escadre* were numbered progressively, but were not identified. Thus GC I/5 had the 1st and 2nd *Escadrilles*, GC II/5 the 3rd and 4th and GC III/5 the 5th and 6th. It was a common practice for the *Escadrilles* to be known by the World War 1 units from which they were descended. For example, the 1st *Escadrille* of GC I/2 was known as Spa 3, and carried the same 'stork' emblem as that carried by the ace Guynemer in World War 1. In the desperate days of May-June 1940, a few makeshift units were formed and used for point defence, being nicknamed by the French 'chimney fighters'. These were designated ECD, *Escadrilles de Chasse de Défense*, and usually had some five or six aircraft. A third category of fighter unit was the ECN (*Escadrille de Chasse de Nuit*), flying nightfighters.

Fighter pilots were given a fairly rigid set of tactical tasks – protection of aircraft in the battle area, protection of ground objectives and destruction of enemy 'expeditions' (sic), i.e. interception. Co-operation with the land forces was on a par with that of the RAF – poor. One of the massive advantages enjoyed by the Wehrmacht was the combined arms attacks which proved so successful in 1940.

In the air, like the RAF, the basic combat unit usually comprised three aircraft, known as a '*patrouille simple*'. Formations were then made up of these three-fighter flights, with nine aircraft, for example, being known as a '*patrouille triple*'. The Germans had long since found that the pair of aircraft gave the best advantage in fighter combat, and this formation was ultimately adopted by the RAF. The French, however, seem not to have drawn the lessons from 1940, and when they resisted the Americans during *Torch*, their opponents commented that 'they used World War 1 tactics'. Once in the RAF, the French pilots used the same techniques as their Allied counterparts.

Colour Plates

1
Hawk 75A-2 '1', s/n 151, flown by *Cne* Jean Accart, GC I/5, Suippes, early 1940

The aircraft has the matricule militaire U-151 under the wings. The number '1' on the fin indicated that this Hawk was the mount of the *escadrille* commander. This is probably the aircraft in which Accart was wounded on 1 June 1940.

2
Hawk 75A-3 '2', s/n 217, flown by Edmond Marin La Meslée, GC I/5, Battle of France

The use of matricule militaires was discontinued after aircraft no 200 was delivered. On the fuselage of this Hawk is the emblem of SPA 67. S/n 217 survived the Battle of France to go to Morocco in 1941, where it received the interim Vichy marking of a white fuselage stripe.

3
Hawk 75A-1 '9', s/n 99, flown by *Sgt* Georges Lemare, GC I/4, France, spring 1940

S/n 99 is seen in typical markings for the period, wearing the emblem of SPA 153 on its fuselage. The small stripe on the fin fillet is a form of rank marking. Note the 30-cm diameter cockades above the wings.

4
Hawk 75A-3 'yellow 67', s/n 267, flown by Camille Plubeau, GC I/5, Morocco (probably Rabat), 1941

Camille Plubeau personal aircraft, this Hawk wears standard green/grey/brown camouflage. On the fuselage is the 'Petit Poucet' badge of GC II/4 (SPA 155), which was Plubeau's old unit, and it is unusually applied in yellow. By the middle of 1942 many of the surviving Vichy Hawks had received a simple grey/brown scheme.

5
Hawk 75A-3 '9', s/n 295, flown by *Sgt* Georges Lemare, *1ere Escadrille* of GC I/4, Dakar-Oukam, September 1941

Not visible in this view is a repeat of the black disc and number on the lower lip of the engine cowling. Shown in standard 1940-style camouflage, the aircraft almost certainly had the grey replaced by a sand colour, although available photos are not absolutely clear on this point.

6
MS.406C-1 '6', s/n 163 (matricule militaire N-483), flown by *Adj* Pierre Le Gloan, *5eme Escadrille* of GC III/6, Chartes, May 1939

Six seems to have been the favourite number of then *Adj* Pierre Le Gloan, who used it on all of his subsequent aircraft as well. This is one of the early MS.406s delivered to the *Armée de l'Air*, for it is fitted with the distinctive Bronzavia exhausts. It was seized by the Italians in November 1942.

7
MS.406C-1 '27', s/n 772 (matricule militaire L-801), flown by *Adj* Klébert Doublet, *2eme Escadrille* of GC III/1, Plessis-Belleville, May 1940

Doublet became an ace on 26 May 1940 when he shot down three aircraft to add to his earlier tally of two. Note the double presentation of SPA 93's duck emblem.

8
MS 406C-1 'III', s/n 948 (matricule militaire L-979), flown by *Sous Lt* Wladyslaw Gnys, *1ere Escadrille* of GC III/1, Norrent-Fontes, 10 May 1940

Gnys scored three shared kills (an He 111 on 12 May and two Do 17s four days later) with GC III/1 to add to his two claims with the Polish Air Force (one of which was the first victory scored by the Poles) to become an ace in mid-May 1940. Marked with the Polish checkerboard, aircraft flown by the Poles in France also seem to have used a system of roman numerals as identifiers.

9
MS.406C-1 '2', s/n 846 (matricule militaire L-875), flown by *Adj* Edgar Gagnaire, *1ere Escadrille* of GC III/1, Rozay-en-Brie, 8 June 1940

Marked with the fox's mask badge of SPA 84, this MS.406 was the mount of *Adj* Edgar Gagnaire on the day he claimed his sixth confirmed kill – a Ju 87. The meaning of the white bar on the fin is not known.

10
MS.406C-1, s/n 819 (matricule militaire L-848), flown by Jean Tulasne, *2eme Escadrille* of GC I/7, Rayak, Syria, December 1940

Jean Tulasne escaped in this aircraft to Palestine from Vichy-controlled Syria. Note the badge of SPA 82 on the fuselage and the Arabic number '1' on the fin.

11
MS.406C-1, s/n 819, flown by James Denis, FAFL GC I 'Alsace', Rayak, Syria, October 1941

Seen almost a year later, s/n 819's cockade has been replaced by the Cross of Lorraine, and most of the tail has been over-painted. Officially, the aircraft had been issued with RAF serial AX864, but it probably never carried it. This aircraft was almost certainly flown by the 1st *Escadrille's* commander, James Denis, during this period.

12
MS.406C-1, s/n 307 (matricule militaire N-819), flown by *Cne* Pierre Pouyade, *Escadrille* 2/595, Tong, French Indo-China (Vietnam), 1942

S/n 307's red tail was a 'neutrality' marking peculiar to Vichy French aircraft operating in the Japanese areas of occupation in South-east Asia. Just forward of the cockpit is the panther emblem of Esc 2/595.

13
Bloch 152C-1 '71', s/n 648, flown by *Cne* Louis Delfino, *4eme Escadrille* of GC II/9, June 1940

Although almost certainly correctly represented here in this profile, sources are contradictory as to the exact fuselage number worn by this aircraft. Delfino himself designed the *Escadrille* emblem on the fin.

14
Bloch 152C-1, s/n 231 (matricule miltaire Y-718), flown by

Cdt Marius Ambrogi, GC I/8, France, mid-1940

This aircraft was flown by 15-kill World War 1 ace Ambrogi, and carried a tricolour band on the fuselage to denote his ace status. He downed a single Do 17 during the Battle of France. The emblem on the aircraft's tail is of 'Dopey', one of Disney's seven dwarves.

15

Bloch 152C-1, s/n 153, flown by Robert Thollon, GC I/8, France, mid-1940

The camouflage worn by this aircraft is typical of the rather dull finish in which most of the Blochs seem to have fought. Thollon scored all eight of his victories during the 1940 campaign, spending the rest of the war as an instructor at a mountain sports training school, while also working closely with the Resistance. He was killed in 1948 in a skiing accident.

16

D.520 '2', s/n 90, flown by Sgt Michel Madon, GC I/3, Oran, North Africa, 1941

Madon was one of the fist pilots to achieve 'acedom' with the D.520, having scored seven kills with GC I/3 by 16 June 1940. He next enjoyed success with the Dewoitine fighter during the Torch landings of 8 November 1942, downing perhaps as many as three C-47s and a single Sea Hurricane on that day. This aircraft is seen some 12 months prior to this action, wearing the distinctive serpent badge of SPA 88.

17

D.520 '6', s/n 277, flown by Pierre Le Gloan, GC III/6, France, June 1940

Le Gloan flew this aircraft in the classic combat on 15 June 1940 in which he shot down four CR.42s and a solitary BR.20. D.520 s/n 277 served Le Gloan well, lasting for over a year, and gaining him ten more kills before finally being written off in a crash-landing in Syria.

18

D.520 '6', s/n 266, flown by Sous Lt René Pomier Leyrargues, GC II/7, France, 5 June 1940

S/n 266 was used by Sous Lt René Pomier Leyrargues to down then ranking German ace, Werner Mölders, on 5 June 1940. Sadly, Leyrargues went to his death not knowing who he had just defeated in aerial combat, for he was in turn shot down in flames by other Bf 109s from III./JG 53 just a matter of minutes later. The panther emblem aft of the cockade was the insignia of SPA 78.

19

D.520 '6', s/n 277, flown by Pierre Le Gloan, GC III/6, Syria, 1941

The same aircraft used so effecetively by Le Gloan against the Italians on 15 June 1940, it is seen here adorned with the all-yellow tail adopted by many Vichy aircraft during the Syrian campaign of 1941 – note also the 'ace stripe' dissecting the white '6' on the fuselage. S/n 277 was written off following air combat with RAF Gladiators from 'X' Flight exactly a year later to the day after downing its five-kill haul. Le Gloan, who claimed one of his opponents destroyed prior to being badly shot up after he had exhausted his ammunition, escaped the forced landing at Rayak without injury.

20

D.520 '6', s/n 300, flown by Pierre Le Gloan, 5eme Escadrille of GC III/6, Algeria, spring 1942

This machine carries the full red and yellow neutrality markings (known as 'the slave's livery') demanded by the Franco-German armistice. Note that the 'ace stripes' now also adorn the wings of this aircraft as well as the fuselage.

21

D.520 'G-G', s/n 347, flown by Gabriel Gauthier, GC II/7, Tunisia, 1942

Marked with his initials, Gauthier had flown this aircraft since the late summer of 1940. It is shown here after it had been repainted with an interesting interpretation of the Vichy stripes on the nose. 'Ace stripes' are also present on the wings of this D.520, as ist the famous stork insignis of SPA 73.

22

D.520 'V', s/n 136, flown by Sous Lt Georges Valentin, 3eme Escadrille of GC II/7, Sidi Ahmed, Tunisia, spring 1942

Also part of GC II/7 at the same time as s/n 347, this older D.520 also bore the initial of its pilot, 11-kill ace Georges Valentin, the stork insignia of SPA 73 and (wider than standard) tricolour 'ace stripes' on the wings.

23

D.520 'G-G', s/n 397, flown by Albert Littolf, FAFL GC III 'Normandie', Rayak, October 1942

This aircraft was salvaged by the mechanics prior to the unit moving to Russia on 11 November, being flown by Albert Littolf on several occasions during this time. This profile is based on interpretations of black and white photos, its colouring appearing to be overall light grey-blue – possibly the standard French underside colour.

24

D.520 'G-G', s/n 347, flown by Gabriel Gauthier, GC II/7, Tunisia, summer 1941

Apart from the red and yellow Vichy markings and the removal of the SPA 73 stork insigne from the fin to below the cockpit, this aircraft retains the same finish it wore in 1940, right down to the fuselage-long white stripe.

25

Potez 631 No 164 (matricule militaire X-933), flown by Pierre Pouyade, ECN IV/13, France, summer 1940

The emblem worn on the nose of this nightfighter is that of C46, which date back to World War 1. Note the white band, originally adopted to differentiate the Potez from the Bf 110 during the Battle of France, which has now been converted into a Vichy-style arrow marking.

26

Spitfire Mk VB BM324, flown by Cdt Bernard Duperier, GC IV/2 'Ile de France'/No 340 Sqn, Hornchurch, 19 August 1942

Flown by Cdt Bernard Duperier, this aircraft carries the special markings adopted by those squadrons participating in the Dieppe operation. It also wears the FAFL Cross of Lorraine and Duperier's personal insignia on standard RAF camouflage of the period. A small letter 'S' was also present under the nose. Issued new to No 340 Sqn in early 1942, this aircraft was used exclusively by them in the frontline, after which it was passed to a series of training units until written on 16 May 1945 when it taxied into a tractor at Tilstock whilst serving with No 81 Operational Training Unit.

27

F-5A Lightning (serial unknown), flown by Antoine de Saint Exupery, 1st *Escadrille* of GR II/33, Bastia, Corsica, Spring 1944

This aircraft was used by Antoine de Saint Exupery, the famous writer-pilot, on several of his lone, long-range, photo-reconnaissance missions over southern France from Corsica. There is some debate as to the colours used on the aircraft of this unit, and it has been shown here in a well-worn standard top surface finish of Olive Drab, with the undersides re-coated in Haze paint. The starboard spinner was a solid dark colour and the name *'Jeanne'*, in script, and crossed pipes appeared on the starboard side of the nose. Note the small tricolour shield mission symbols. below the forward camera port.

28

Tempest Mk V NV994, flown by flown by Flt Lt P H Clostermann, No 3 Sqn, Hopsten (B.112), April 1945

Delivered to No 3 Sqn on 15 April 1945, NV994 was coded 'JF-E' and frequently flown by 'A' Flight commander, Flt Lt Pierre Clostermann. On 20 April he destroyed two Fw 190s in one sortie in this aircraft. NV994 was declared 'Cat B' on 1 July 1945 (cause not known) and repaired by Hawker Aircraft at Langley. It was then stored at No 20 Maintenance Unit (MU) at Aston Down until April 1950, when it was returned to Hawker Aircraft for conversion to TT 5 (target-tug) standard. Issued in April 1952 to Sylt Armament Practice Station (APS), it served as 'D' until October 1954, when it went into store at No 20 MU again, before finally being sold back to the manufacturers in July 1955.

29

Hurricane Mk I (Trop) Z4797, flown by Jean Tulasne and probably Albert Littolf, FAFL GC I *'Alsace'*, Fuka, Western Desert, May 1942

This aircraft is finished in standard RAF Tropical Scheme camouflage, adorned with Free French markings and a tricolour spinner. Z4797 was passed to GC I after service with No 80 Sqn, the aircraft returning to RAF control following its time with the French to serve with No 26 Anti-Aircraft Cooperation Unit. It was finally Struck off Charge on 1 February 1944.

30

Hurricane Mk II (Trop) 'S' (serial unknown), flown by Lt Camille Plubeau, possibly from the fighter school at Meknes, Morocco, 1944

The heavily worn and touched up paintwork which adorned this veteran fighter effectively hid its serial. Although not formally identified, the emblem on the fin was probably that of the fighter school at Meknes, which Plubeau commanded between February and November 1944.

31

Yak-1 '44', flown by Marcel Albert, GC III *'Normandie'*, Ivanovo, Russia, April 1943

Usually flown by Marcel Albert, this aircraft is finished in temporary VVS winter camouflage, with the addition of a small French cockade under the windscreen.

32

Yak-1 '11', flown by Albert Durand, GC III *'Normandie'*, Orel, Russia, May 1943

The aircraft had a blotched and faded appearance, which may have been caused by the remains of a temporary winter camouflage. So far as is known, this was the only Yak with the unit to carry a sharksmouth.

33

Yak-9 '14', flown by Marcel Lefèvre, GC III *'Normandie'*, Sloboda, Russia, October 1943

Lefèvre's aircraft carries the lightning flash seen on many of the unit's Yaks at this time. *'La Pére Magloire'* also wears 11 crosses, indicating kills – a marking never used by Soviet pilots.

34

Yak-9 '60', flown by René Challe, GC III *'Normandie'*, Dubrovka, Russia, June 1944

Shown in grey camouflage, which was beginning to be introduced at about this time, this aircraft was flown by René Challe, the CO of the 4e *Escadrille 'Caen'*. It wears the 'fury' emblem of the 6e *Escadrille* of GC III/7, his old unit in France.

35

Yak-9 '5', flown by Roger Sauvage, GC III *'Normandie'*, Toula, Russia, May 1944

Shown here finished in a grey camouflage pattern, this aircraft was Sauvage's mount for much of the summer of 1944.

36

Yak-9 'Yellow 35', flown by Jacques André, GC III *'Normandie'*, Toula, Russia, winter 1943-44

This aircraft had its identifying number painted in yellow, rather than the more common white. André was one of the leading French aces on the Eastern Front, and was also a Hero of the Soviet Union gold star winner.

37

Yak-3 '1', flown by René Challe, *1ere Escadrille 'Rouen'* of GC III *'Normandie-Niémen'*, East Prussia, December 1944-17 January 1945

Like other French aces in-theatre, Challe also chose to record his kills with German crosses. His Russian counterparts refused to desecrate their aircraft with such decorations.

38

Yak-3 '6', flown by Marcel Albert, GC III *'Normandie-Niémen'*, East Prussia, late 1944

Remarkbly, this aircraft was never hit by enemy fire throughout its long, and action-packed, history as the mount of the leading ace of the *'Normandie-Niemen'*. With 22 kills shown, the Yak-3 is depicted in profile in late 1944.

39

FK.58 '11', S/N 11, in service with *Ecole de Chasse* at Lyon-Bron or Montpellier after the June 1940 Armistic

Although ordered in quantity, the FK.58 was a victim of the disorganisation within the European aircraft industry of the time, being delivered piecemeal, and therefore seeing little action. Possibly their most useful function was to prepare Polish pilots, who were then under training on the Dutch fighter at the time of the armistice, for the more modern aircraft that some of them would fly with the RAF.

Back cover profile
MS.406 s/n 1019 (matricule militaire L-609), flown by *Général* Armand Pinsard as a hack, France, October 1939
Wearing an all-black finish on the fuselage uppersurfaces, s/n 1019 (nicknamed 'The Pirate') bears the emblem of SPA 26. Pinsard scored 27 kills in World War 1, and commanded *Groupement de Chasse* 21 in World War 2 until 6 June 1940, when he lost a leg in a bombing raid.

FIGURE PLATES

1
Sous-Lieutenant Edmond Marin La Meslée of GC I/5 is depicted in late 1939 wearing the 'Louise blue' uniform of the *Armée de l'Air*, with the alternate breeches and riding boots. Note his pilots' badge on his right breast pocket. The embroidered wings above them is La Meslée's 'speciality' badge, indicating his aircrew status.

2
Sous-Lieutenant Pierre Le Gloan of GC III/6. He is depicted in summer issue flying gear at Athens-Eleusis in May 1941, en route to Syria. Le Gloan is wearing a white shirt with rank insignia on the shoulders, black tie, light khaki coloured shorts, long white socks and black shoes. His cap is that of the *Armée de l'Air*, with a white summer top and a single gold band indicating his rank.

3
Commandant Pierre Pouyade, third CO of GC III, the *Normandie-Niémen* Regiment in Russia in 1943-44. He is wearing his blue *Armée de l'Air* service cap, a British Irvine sheepskin flying jacket and VVS khaki breeches, with black boots.

4
Capitaine Alois Vasatko was a Czech ace flying with GC I/5 during the Battle of France. His uniform is French issue, but his cap band carries the Czech badge, indicating his combatant status. He is also wearing the short black leather jacket, which was popular with French aircrew both before and during the war.

5
Sous-Lieutenant Georges Pissotte of GC III/2 in the winter of 1939-40. He is clothed in the standard French fighter pilot's flying suit and cumbersome rigid leather flying helmet of the period. Not shown on his person is the bulky chest-mounted oxygen regulator or the radio connections, both of which he would need in flight.

6
Commandant Bernard Duperier of GC IV/2 *'Île de France'/* No 340 Sqn between May 1942 and January 1943. He wears his French uniform and rank insignia, along with the ribbon of the DFC, RAF wings and his prized French 'macaron'. His flying apparel is completed by a pair of standard 1936 Pattern RAF flying boots, leather gloves and the obligatory 'fighter-type' silk scarf.

BIBLIOGRAPHY

Airdoc, L'Aviation Militaire Française d'Armistice
Avions, Le Morane Saulnier MS 406
Brindley, J. F., French Fighters of World War Two
Christienne, C., Histoire de l'Aviation Militaire Française
Cuich, M. N., Guynemer et ses Avions
Cuny, J & Beauchamp, G., Curtiss Hawk 75
Curtiss Aircraft Co, Notice d'Entretien et de Reparation de l'Avion Curtiss H-75A-4
Danel, R & Cuny, J, L'Aviation de Chasse Française 1918-1940
Danel, R & Cuny, J, Le Dewoitine D.520
Decock, J. P., Normandie-Niémen du Yak au Mirage
Editions DTU, Dewoitine D520
Ehrengardt, C-J, L'Aviation de Vichy au Combat (2 vols)
Facon, P, L'Armée de l'Air dans la Tourmente
Forty, G & Duncan, J, The Fall of France
Gaujour, R, French Air Force 1940-1944
Halley, J. J., Squadrons of the RAF & Commonwealth 1918-1988
Horne, A., To Lose a Battle. France 1940
IPMS France, Bloch 152
Jackson, R., Airwar over France
Lambert, J. W., Wildcats over Casablanca
Martin, P., Invisibles Vainquers

Morgan, H., Aircraft of the 15 - Soviet Aces of World War 2
Porret, D & Thevenet, F., Les As de la Guerre 1939-1945 (2 vols)
Potier, P. & Pernet, J., Historique de la Base 113
Roger, F. & P., Combats Aeriens sur La Meuse & La Semoy 10-14 Mai 1940
Salesse, Lt Col, L'Aviation de Chasse Française en 1939-40
Shores, C. & Williams, C., Aces High
Shores, C., Dust Clouds in the Middle East
Shores, C., Fledgling Eagles
Soumille, A., L'Aviation Militaire Française dans la Bataille de France
Van Haute, A., Pictorial History of the French Air Force (2 vols)

Articles in numerous issues of the following periodicals:
Aero Journal
Avions
Camouflage Air Journal
Fanatique de l'Aviation
IPMS France Journal
Icare
Profiles
Replic